JESS INDEEDY

List yourself happy

100 Lists to Inspire Real Change

Illustrations by Basia Stryjecka

Hardie Grant

QUADRILLE

Contents

Introduction

I'm so glad you're here!

List-making for self-improvement has been a part of my life since I was in my early teens. I've found such peace and fulfilment from organizing my thoughts into lists, whether it be goal-setting, taking stock or arranging ideas from my imagination.

I believe that the practice of list-making can truly increase your happiness and life satisfaction, and all of the lists in this book have been created to help you achieve just that.

I've always loved making lists with other people, and comparing our entries to find how uniquely each of our brains work, and to notice those familiar undercurrents of the sameness that is human nature. In fact, I created the world's first list-making night, I Love Lists, for this reason. These evenings were magical – as the compère, I provided the structure and set the list topics, and guests open-heartedly shared their entries with the room. The communal sense of self-discovery was palpable, and everyone left with a to-do list to turn their findings into reality. I Love Lists is the inspiration for this book, a way to achieve this magical discovery through the power of lists in the comfort of your own home.

I am writing this book with you in mind, and we are making these lists together. I've shared my own personal thoughts with each list in the hope that my openness inspires you to come up with your own entries in the most honest way. What you put into your list-making sessions is what you'll get out of them, so let your imagination and inner truths run free.

Most of the list topics I've included have been inspired by psychological and scientific research on happiness and life satisfaction. My superpower is in organizing these findings in a fun, inspiring way to help you draw out your unique expression of happiness.

One of the best parts about the list content I've included in this book is that it is 'evergreen'. As your capacity for happiness grows, your list entries and actions will evolve. You can make the same ten lists one year apart, and wonder at the difference in your answers.

I hope this book becomes a covetable part of your happiness practice, and an accompaniment on your journey of the ever-evolving, beautiful expression that is your life.

With love and lists,

How this book works

This book is designed to extract your 'inner gold' to help you bring your unique values, dreams and ideas into your everyday life for optimum happiness. I recommend you schedule in a list-making session at least monthly, choosing ten lists from the book, and complete the related action steps within the month.

I've given you some suggested 'recipes' for your ten lists to complete for the month. You can follow my recipes, or choose ten lists of your own.

The process of making the lists, choosing one action step from each list, and adding them to your plan for the month, results in incremental improvement. You should feel inspired, rather than overloaded, from this process because it's been broken down into achievable bite-sized tasks. By you! Of course, if you're an overachiever like me, you'll be tempted to rush through all the lists at once. But don't forget, this book's aim is to help you increase your happiness. And happiness is a practice, not a race.

What you'll need

- A dedicated notebook, app or document to hold all your excellent list-making work.

- A calendar or diary to schedule in your tasks.

- An open mind and heart, and a dedication to a regular happiness practice!

List recipes

To help you get started, I've created some combinations
of lists that are themed, or balanced with the cornerstones
of happiness, or vary in degrees of 'work'.

These lists are just suggestions, in case you want some direction.
You can, of course, choose your own list-making adventures!

The Basics: 4, 15, 17, 21, 27, 28, 46, 76, 92, 99

Invigorate: 8, 38, 39, 40, 44, 47, 49, 52, 74, 86

Have Fun: 14, 18, 22, 36, 48, 51, 57, 66, 93, 98

Relax: 1, 31, 54, 65, 67, 78, 81, 82, 94, 95

Bliss Bootcamp: 9, 41, 45, 60, 68, 69, 79, 80, 82, 83

Reach For The Stars: 2, 6, 20, 33, 70, 73, 75, 85, 88, 89

Know Thyself: 5, 11, 12, 19, 34, 35, 71, 72, 96, 100

Connect: 3, 23, 55, 56, 58, 59, 61, 62, 63, 84

Evolve: 16, 24, 25, 26, 29, 30, 50, 77, 87, 91

Dream: 7, 10, 13, 32, 37, 42, 43, 53, 90, 97

How to

Set aside an hour for your monthly list-making session. Try to limit your distractions during this time, perhaps by turning off phone notifications and telling your family or housemates that you're going to be unavailable for an hour.

Choose ten lists, either by using my 'recipes' or by selecting your own. I recommend you chose a variety of different lists to vary the level of 'work'.

Each list is set into two parts. The first is the list topic, with guidance and examples from me. You'll make a list based on the topic and instructions, and here is where I urge you to speak your truth, your wildest dreams and your deepest emotions.

The second part is the action plan, where you'll take your findings from your entries and turn them into reality. I'll ask you to schedule time in for things, or to set deadlines for certain tasks. Choose one action step from the list to complete within the next month. You will end up with a workable list of ten action steps, planned into your calendar, decided by you for your own ultimate happiness.

If the action step part sounds daunting, don't worry – you've already done the hard work in part one, which is chronicling your inner thoughts on the subject. Now all you have to do is take action!

OVERVIEW

1

Choose ten list topics.

2

Work through each of the ten lists, writing down
your entries and subsequent action steps.

3

Choose one action step from each list, and
achieve these ten goals in the next month.

4

Repeat the above process the following month,
choosing ten different list topics.

Let's begin!

1

Nature is a healer

In our modern fast-paced lives, it can be easy to forget to take in the beauty of the natural world. Whether we notice or not, we're surrounded by ever-thriving, life-giving nature.

Spending time in nature makes us feel more connected to the world around us, and getting plenty of fresh air is good for your mood. The Japanese practice of shinrin-yoku, or 'forest bathing', is proven to reduce stress levels and has countless health benefits, such as improved sleep and increased energy. Surrounding ourselves with trees, we thrive from the higher levels of oxygen that exist in a forest, rather than in a city, and they emit plant chemicals called phytoncides, which have been proven to lower blood pressure and boost your mood. Stepping away from our technology and being 'in the moment' are also sure-fire ways to increase levels of happiness and life-satisfaction.

List ten ways you can add more nature into your life.

Your list entries could include bringing more nature into your home, exercise regime, self-care, or focus on spending more time outdoors.

For example, you could go for a brisk walk in a local park or forest once a week, perhaps inviting a friend to join you (for a happiness extra credit!). Surround yourself with glorious chlorophyll by visiting your local garden centre and buying some pet plants for your home. Pick up an array of flowers from your local florist and spend some quiet time arranging them in your own personal style. Gather foliage on one of your walks to make a decorative seasonal tablescape or wreath.

You could even engage in some 'rogue gardening' by planting some flowers into a bare patch in your neighbourhood, and lovingly tend them. The possibilities are endless!

 **TAKE ACTION**

Choosing from the items on your list, schedule in one hour per week during the next month to embrace nature.

Think about what parts of these experiences will be most fulfilling for your senses – the lovely scent of pine trees, the beauty of rolling green hills or the feeling of fresh air on your skin. When you're engaging in your nature sessions, take time to consciously enjoy these sensory aspects.

When I go for walks, I love to bask in all of the shades of green on the tree leaves, fluffy grass and mossy patches. I take deep breaths of the fresh air that I know they're contributing to. No matter the season, I like to take my shoes off and put my bare feet on the ground and feel connected to the earth. Our planet is so beautiful, and we can all spend more time appreciating it.

2

Creative challenge

Creative expression helps us process our emotions, experience joy and embrace beauty. I regard the act of being creative as a form of self-care – I love getting lost in my various projects and it feels so luxurious. Even if you work in a creative industry like me, it's important to express yourself through art, music, making and dance, for your own sake. I want you to have fun with this list!

If you had plenty of time to get creative every day, what would you do? Make a list of ten creative activities that come to mind.

Be very specific here. Instead of simply listing the word 'dancing', perhaps add 'look up tutorials on YouTube for Beyoncé music video dance routines'. If you add 'painting' to your list, it could perhaps be expanded to 'paint some watercolour thank-you notes'. An entry of 'cake decorating' can be made more fun with 'decorating a cake to portray a jungle scene'. Being specific about these activities will help you actually do them.

Everyone has their own preferences on how they get creative. For me, I'm drawn to making music, designing stage costumes, cooking and baking, and crafting. I have a bunch of musical instruments at home, and I write music, learn how to play my favourite songs and sometimes I play along with music on the radio just for fun. I love to make costumes for myself, my husband and my dog. Writing this entry reminds me that I haven't spent nearly enough time with my glue gun lately!

Try to transcend your usual creative outlets on this list to include things you haven't tried before, because variety is the sweet spice of this cake called life.

 **TAKE ACTION**

Choose a creative activity from your list and set aside one hour per week in the next month to devote to it.

Make it a priority to set aside time for your creative expression, as a part of your self-care routine. Be vigilant to honour this time for yourself.

This action step is meant to feel enjoyable, and even indulgent. You don't have to do a different creative activity every time, for instance, you could indulge in weekly sessions of watercolour painting and become more masterful at the medium. This will still have the desired effect of your creative expression leading to improved happiness, and it is a great way to start.

However, I do recommend adding some new creative outlets to this exercise, because you never know what you'll discover about yourself! Recently I've become interested in making my own aromatherapy mixtures and I was surprised to find how much fun it is to make my own scents. It's like a new world of sensory possibilities has been unlocked!

3

Take care of your patch

You've heard the adage 'think globally, act locally'. Can you imagine if everybody followed this mindset, how quickly a local improvement could become a global one?

This list is all about your local community and neighbourhood. Being active in your community and helping improve your area gives you a sense of belonging, which is a primal human need and is key to life satisfaction.

What would make your city or neighbourhood even better?

Write down all the ways you can improve your own personal experience of your patch, but also think of those less privileged than you. How can you help your area be a better place for others? Take into account your personal values, and how you'd like to see them mirrored in your community. Maybe there's a littering problem, making your neighbourhood feel neglected. Perhaps there aren't any community events taking place, which would provide space for locals to get to know each other and feel a true belonging to their area.

As an environmentalist, I would love my neighbourhood to have a better set-up for compost waste and its collection. Also, I'm lucky to live near a park with a basketball court, but it's always covered in leaves and the nets are always old and broken. I love to shoot hoops, but I also know there are lots of kids in my neighbourhood who would benefit from that basketball court to be fully functional at all times.

TAKE ACTION

Choose one of your improvements and commit to taking action on this during the next month.

For instance, if it's the litter problem you'd like to solve, challenge yourself to pick up three pieces of litter every day, or arrange a community litter pick for one hour during the next month. Even better, look online for local community groups to join, as you might find an anti-litter initiative already exists in your area.

Look for local community events in your area to attend, and try to meet people who live nearby while you're there. Assess how these events could better serve your community, perhaps by better representation or more engaging and inclusive activities. If there are no community events listed anywhere, talk to your local council to find out if they have any planned – perhaps you can join the planning committee!

For my green dreams, I'd contact my local council to request more communal compost bins, and ask them to remind residents that composting is encouraged. I'd also find out how the basketball court in my neighbourhood is managed, and look into getting help in improving its upkeep. Perhaps I'd start an action group of local basketball enthusiasts and we can pledge to look after the court ourselves. And the added bonus is I'd make some new friends with similar interests!

4

Declutter your mind

We live in trying times, our collective mental health is at risk, and that blessing and curse of the internet has us comparing ourselves to unrealistic depictions of celebrities, gurus and even our peers. Looking after our happiness hygiene is more important than ever!

We all tend to carry around worries and unhelpful scripts in our daily thoughts. Sometimes anxiety can be helpful in preparing you for something you're worrying about, but sometimes you get stuck in a loop of needless worries about things that are simply out of your control. This kind of thinking holds you back.

I have great news! Writing down these concerns somewhat magically helps you sort out which of these thoughts are holding you back, and which can be classified as 'useful anxiety'. And then, after writing it all down, you can figure out what you need to declutter and what needs more careful attention.

Make a list of the things that have been troubling you, making you lose sleep or issues you have hang-ups about.

Quickly jot down the first thoughts that come to mind, because those are likely the ones that are bothering you the most. These can include annoying patterns in your life, bad habits, recurring issues and fears. Get it all out, because we're going to let it all go!

I make this list when I'm stuck in a rut, or if I have a string of perceived 'bad luck'. Seeing my hang-ups on paper is eye-opening, as I tend to exaggerate things that really don't deserve so much of my headspace. A spring clean for the mind!

TAKE ACTION

Make an action plan for one item on the list and attack it this month to get the worry off your plate, or at least work towards improving the situation.

Circle which of the items on your list are within your control, and write down what steps you can take to eradicate these worries from your life.

Cross out the items on your list that are out of your control, and cast them out of your mind.

You might even find the strength you gain from facing one particular worry on your list this month will give you incredible power to squash the other items. Or perhaps you'll realize the things that have been taking up your mental and emotional energy just don't deserve it!

Often I look at my list of troubles and instantly berate myself for not realizing how privileged I am to be worrying about such trivial stuff. Writing this list always reminds me to be grateful, and that I could be putting my energy to better use.

5

What makes you happy

We spend a lot of time thinking that things like money, success, inanimate objects or our appearance play a big role in our happiness, but they don't. It's been proven in various psychological studies that experiences make us the most happy, rather than a new Lamborghini. This list will help you unlock what makes you truly happy, in your own flavour.

Reflect, consult your heart and make a list of what brings you true happiness.

It may be helpful to reflect on times when you've felt particularly happy, whether it be for a week or a moment. What aspects of these experiences made you feel happiness? Were you with family or friends? Were you witnessing beauty or nature? Perhaps you think of something more recent, like seeing an adorable dog in your neighbourhood which gave you an instant serotonin buzz.

For me, I'm at my happiest when I'm spending time with the people I love and having fun, meaningful shared experiences. Often this is centred around food and cooking, travelling and singing karaoke. I love the quiet happy heart hum I get when I'm together with my family and friends, just existing together. I can also find a font of happiness on my own – I feel so fulfilled experiencing art and listening to music, learning new things and losing myself in creative projects.

TAKE ACTION

From your happiness list, add one of these aspects to your life on a weekly basis for the next month.

The plans you make for this task should feel delicious, and moments that you're really looking forward to. The regular practice of adding these things into your life will not only make you feel instantly happier, but will also transform your long-term life satisfaction.

For instance, if it was the cute pup you saw in your neighbourhood that lifted your spirits, perhaps you could join a dog-borrowing service, or volunteer at a local shelter for some canine cuddle time. Or adopt a rescue dog for unlimited joy!

My action plan would involve contacting friends and family and make plans to spend some time together, to get that happy heart hum. I'd research and book some exciting travel for the year ahead, and invite some people I love so we can make wonderful memories. I'd definitely treat myself to some Spotify karaoke, which is a tried and tested way for me to feel joy!

6

How would you like to be described?

This exercise is like writing your own compliments, except all of these are the ones you really want to hear! It can be easy to experience the world reactively without thinking about what we add to it. We can't control how we're perceived, but we can control how we present ourselves.

This list guides you towards clarifying your values and what you truly want to share with the world. You can actually be this person right now, just start by 'walking the talk' and people's perceptions will follow!

Make a list of all the ways you'd like to be described.

Feel free to use adjectives, nouns, adverbs, exclamation marks! You're wonderful, gorgeous, a hoot! You can list qualities that are valuable in relationships such as reliable, loving, a good listener, or professional qualities such as being a good leader, or personal ones such as thoughtful, talented, a great cook.

Personally, I always want be thought of as helpful, inspiring, creative, intelligent and successful. I feel so proud when someone says I'm a good friend, or that I helped them, or if I've inspired someone to be creative or to succeed.

TAKE ACTION

Write down your pathways to become more like the person in your descriptions, and complete one task from a pathway this month.

What actions do you need to take to get closer to this version of yourself?

For example, if you wanted to be described as 'successful', what would that look like? Perhaps you'd think of a certain annual income, or to have a wardrobe full of gorgeous suits, or maybe earn some awards and accolades in your industry? One pathway you could pursue is by doing some research on awards in your industry and how to get nominated. And as RuPaul once said, 'You wanna make more money? Wear a suit'.

My personal pathways to become more like the person in my description could include releasing an online course so that I can help even more people find true happiness. Perhaps I could focus on increasing my social media following and my network in order to reach and inspire a larger audience. If I wanted to be perceived as more intelligent, I could read more books about a chosen subject, or add more university lecturing to my experience.

I think you're just fantastic!

7

Wouldn't it be great if...?

This is a free writing, imaginative list that will reveal areas of your life and the world that you feel need improving. The casual wording of this list should put you at ease, and in a positive frame of mind to dream. I learned about this mindset prompt from business mentor Marie Forleo, and I regularly make it into a list.

In addition to helping me imagine a better world or a more enjoyable life, it helps me find solutions to things that are inconvenient or annoying. Sometimes my entries for this list are futuristic technological ideas and life hacks that don't exist yet. Maybe I'm sitting on a goldmine!

Wouldn't it be great if... you listed out all the things you think could improve your life, others' lives or the world around you.

These entries don't need to be realistic. Let yourself dream.

For instance, wouldn't it be great if I could live and work in New Zealand for a year? Wouldn't it be great if I had a wardrobe full of cool clothes I was really proud of? Wouldn't it be great if my favourite restaurant opened in my area? Wouldn't it be great if I could train my dog to bring me coffee?

I often make this list aloud, in conversation with my husband Charles, and we try to life hack ways to turn my ideas into reality. It always turns into a really creative brainstorm.

TAKE ACTION

Write down what steps you can take to make these ideas happen, and choose one step to complete this month.

Assess which of these ideas you can turn into reality yourself, by asking for help, outsourcing or researching some solutions. Some of your ideas might not be actionable now, so choose one that is and write down the steps to make it happen.

For the more reality-based ideas I suggested, you could research visas, jobs and plane tickets to find out how entirely possible it would be to achieve the New Zealand dream.

For your dream wardrobe, you could go through your clothes and pick out the things you do like, and declutter the stuff that's not your style. If you love that restaurant enough to want it to open in your area, it's probably worth the effort to travel to it now and then.

I know I'll never train my dog to bring me coffee, but the concept really did get my wheels turning!

8

What would you do if you had more time?

We need to make time for the things that are really important to us. With all of the distractions available to us these days (thanks, technology) it's too easy to procrastinate and prioritize things that don't really make us happy. Life can be short, so let's be more mindful about how we spend our time.

Make a list of all the things you would do if you were given a bonus hour each day.

Perhaps you've got a personal project that you've been putting off, or your windows desperately need cleaning. Maybe you wish you had more time for exercise or to see your friends.

If I were given a bonus hour, I'd want to spend it doing the fun, creative things I always put off, because they can often seem incidental to my default focus, which tends to be on my business and my health (exercise, sleep, food, sunlight). I could always spend more time playing with my dog, who always makes time for me.

I know I'd sleep better, and have a lot more fun if I just let myself indulge in these things!

TAKE ACTION

Choose an item from your list that you feel would truly improve your life and happiness, and make time for it by scheduling it in this month.

Clear the time in your calendar, and make it non-negotiable. Tell your family, partner or housemates that you're planning on engaging in this project or activity and that you won't want to be disturbed. If you're struggling to find spare time, is there anything superfluous you can cut out of your day to make room? If it feels impossible, you should reflect on why you aren't making time for yourself now.

If you wrote 'exercise more', perhaps you could go to bed an hour earlier and wake up an hour earlier to get your sweat on. You could cut out the half an hour of scrolling through social media and do a fun online workout instead. Feel free to innovate for yourself – I always do squats while I'm brushing my teeth and leg stretches in front of the TV in the evening.

If you're feeling really time-poor, you could delegate household chores to someone, or just do the dishes tomorrow so you can do the yoga now. Be careful not to 'protaskinate', which the habit of doing mundane chores instead of the more important things!

9

Ten luxurious ways to spoil yourself

Self-care should be a part of our daily routine, and it has been a popular subject of countless articles in recent years. This list aims to transcend your basic self-care with a view to upgrading how well you treat yourself. There is a lot of scientific research about the human response to rewards, and how it helps people stay on track with their goals. So by taking such good care of yourself, you'll have a far better chance of achieving your dreams!

We can learn a lot from the style in which we choose to spoil ourselves and luxuriate. Turning these luxuries into a regular routine makes us feel really looked after, and needn't be 'expensive' – an hour-long bath twice a week with candles and music costs next to nothing.

If you engage your creativity in this exercise and make yourself feel completely spoiled, it will in turn reinforce a sense of high self-worth and that you deserve all the wonderful successes of your life. These sentiments feed into each other for infinity in a never-ending loop of happiness.

Make a list of ten ways to treat yourself in a luxurious fashion.

I've been making this list for about five years, and I can tell you it's all about mindset. Sometimes we have to dare to luxuriate! Everyone has their own personal style of spoiling themselves. Perhaps you'd like to be fed grapes while you get a foot massage, or you treat yourself to a vintage silk kimono, or book a week-long yoga retreat on a Mediterranean island.

My daring luxuries include having my favourite scented candles in every room of the house, an unlimited budget for buying books (as long as I read them) and having regular aromatherapy massages.

 **TAKE ACTION**

Schedule in at least three of the luxurious activities on your list to your calendar this month.

If some of the items on your list break the bank, then plan them for the long term as rewards for your achievements. You can also create versions of your entries to fit your budget and make them more accessible to you now.

What may be interesting is a quick analysis of why you chose certain items on this list. Perhaps you're seeking grape-fed relaxation because you're feeling stressed, overworked or tired. Maybe it will provide some insight about how you're taking care of yourself on a day-to-day basis and help nudge you in the direction of a more self-care led lifestyle.

10

The best party ever!

The creative expression of planning your dream party, with no budgetary restrictions, really makes your imagination flow. This list will help you think of amazing ways to blow off steam, celebrate with your loved ones and make unforgettable memories.

Imagine you have an unlimited budget, and make a list of all the elements you'd plan for the party of your dreams.

Write down who you'd invite, what your senses would experience, how you would feel afterwards, what would make it over-the-top. Dream big!

For this list, find more inspiration in the details by imagining the guests' experience from receiving the invitation all the way to their feeling the day after. Be sure to engage all of the senses as you plan the best party ever: what it looks like, sounds like, smells like... What does the experience feel like? What food and drink will be served? You can involve various themes, and imagine different settings and venues. Have you planned your outfit yet?

An interesting side-effect of this list is that it indicates what you really need in your life. Is it love, excitement, more friends, or do you just need a great party? You definitely deserve it!

As an event designer, I often daydream about this list. Sometimes I use it as a planning tool – I initially dream really big about a client's event and then downscale it to match their budget.

It definitely gets my creativity flowing, because my mind tries to find practical solutions for making my big ideas happen.

TAKE ACTION

Take elements from this list and add them to your next party or celebration.

Look at your diary for birthdays, holidays or anniversaries in the next month, and plan and plug in ideas from your list. Gather your most fun friends and plan an epic event. Give your niece or nephew the princess party of their dreams, recreate a party from a foregone decade, and plan the menu, music and dress code with historical accuracy, utilize your passion for cinema and throw an Oscars party, and invite your most fabulous friends.

You can also apply this party practice to everyday life, because any day is a good excuse to celebrate.

Once I was hired to create a yacht-themed party, except there was no yacht, no sea, no sun in sight. The event was held in a private indoor event space, so I added every obvious element I could to make the party as nautical as possible. I built a small-scale yacht façade for the DJ booth, made decorations that looked like ocean waves and jumping fish, and piped in scents from diffusers, including coconut to invoke the smell of suntan lotion. I added some fun accessories like captain's caps, and brightly coloured cocktails, and we were sailing!

11

Feelings!

This list can be used in regular practice for a healthier mental hygiene around feeling your emotions. Putting your feelings into words helps you better manage them, it allows you to empathize with yourself, and channel your focus towards the emotions you really want to feel.

Think back over the day and make a list of all the feelings you've felt so far today.

Start from when you woke up to right now. Assign a feeling to each thought, circumstance, issue, interaction. When you got out of bed, perhaps you felt energized and excited for the day, or a bit forlorn and rickety. Maybe you had a stressful journey into work and feared you'd be late, or you had an easy stroll to the office and saw a beautiful rose bush on the way.

As you make your list, re-feel the feelings for better self-awareness and to help you know what to work towards.

For me, today I've had a positive feeling of joy, trust and love, when my dog bounded up onto the bed to greet me this morning.

Maybe today you woke up with positive anticipation for this list-making session!

TAKE ACTION

Assess if there were any negative feelings you'd like to replace with more positive ones in the future. Consider where the negative feelings stemmed from – it could be from lack of preparation, not enough food, water or sleep, or perhaps you just let yourself feel yucky and forgot to try to snap out of it.

If you woke up feeling stressed and rushed around, you could set your alarm earlier and do something nice for yourself with the extra time. Things like meditation, going for some outdoor exercise or having a bath instead of a shower will surely set you up for a brighter day! You have more control than you think in managing your feelings, so let's try to feel good.

I took more time to cuddle my dog Marlowe, which instantly boosted my mood and gratitude! These actions I took towards my own life enjoyment not only worked for today, but I know they will help me get stronger in taking better care of my happiness in the future.

12

List your strengths and talents

There are lots of studies that show a person's happiness and life satisfaction are greater if they regularly use their personal strengths and talents. We simply feel better by doing things we're good at, and everything we do always comes out better if we've enjoyed ourselves in the process. Imagine if we built our days, careers and relationships with this in mind? We'd all be positively flourishing. Let's do it!

Make a list of your personal strengths and talents.

You should know a few right off the bat, because you've been complimented on these strengths or talents in the past. Also, I'm pretty sure you know how you're blessed. If you struggle to come up with items for your list, you can scan through your mind for achievements, praise and experiences from your past. Perhaps there was a subject at school you excelled at, or a certain skill that you picked up quickly and enjoyed using. Perhaps you're a caring friend, or good at sports, or you've got the gift of the gab.

One of my strengths is humour, and when I use my sense of humour with friends and family it brings levity to any awkward situations and helps everyone bond. I know that when I watch comedy and read books or articles that are funny, my mood is definitely brighter.

Another one of my natural passions is learning, simply for learning's sake – I absolutely love taking courses and researching things. I don't need for there to be a use or application for what I'm learning, I just love to learn!

 **T A K E   A C T I O N**

Use one talent from your list each week for the next month to highlight your strengths.

Refer to your list and think about how can you regularly use these gifts in your life. What can you add into your life to make the most of your wonderful self, and share it with others?

If you were commended for your poetry at school, you could write some poetry this month and let your creativity flow. If you're good at sports, get out and get playing. If you've got the gift of the gab, you're probably gabbing away already, but maybe you can use this superpower to help a cause you really care about.

I use my humour strength in every corner of my life, from cheering up friends to cracking jokes on stage to my event audiences. Luckily for me there are endless ways of learning, and I've taken all sorts of courses in person and online. From a 'Creative Vegetables' course at Le Cordon Bleu to Neil Gaiman's creative writing Masterclass, I devour it all. I'm currently learning piano online from a teacher in Canada. My skill for learning also helps me share information with others, which has made writing this book so enjoyable.

13

Wish list

A genie has appeared and they've generously given you ten wishes. You can wish for anything except for unlimited wishes (dang it!). What would you wish for?

This list gives us insight into how we'd each architect our world, and our deep sense of what needs to be fixed. Some of our wishes will be unachievable in our lifetimes, but that doesn't stop us from building towards them and leaving our legacy. Using our creativity to come up with these wishes and taking actions towards making them real will increase our sense of autonomy over our future.

Make a list of ten wishes you'd ask your generous genie.

If it helps you flow, make a free-list of 20/30/40 wishes and select a final ten afterwards.

You could wish for anything from monetary gains or true love to technological advancement. You can even ask for unlimited marshmallows, but remember you only have ten of these wishes, so spend them wisely!

My wish list always asks for world peace, ending hunger, and the end of the patriarchy and systemic racism. My other entries are pretty variable and depend on my overall life satisfaction at the time, the season, what I'm reading and what I'm watching.

Often this list gives me clues on how I can help others, and what areas of my life need attention. For instance, I felt the urge to make a simple fun wish list today, which means I probably need a break and to add some fun into my life!

One of the things I'd wish for today would be to live in a big country house in a sunny part of France, with enough room for all my family and friends to stay when they visit. It's a dreary day in London and I haven't seen my friends and family in ages, so I'm not surprised this entry landed on my list today!

 **TAKE ACTION**

Choose one of your wishes, and assign a task to complete in the next month to achieve it or bring it closer to reality.

How can you turn items from your wish list into reality, even in a small way? Assess your entries and see if there is a common theme between any of them. What do these wishes say about your values? Did you learn something new about yourself? What was the tone – were these lists silly and fun, or aspirational, or sober and principled?

For example, my 'house in sunny France' entry might inspire me to make more regular plans with my friends and family, and to schedule in a summer holiday. While my wish to live in a big house in a sunny part of the country is a bit of a leap, it is not impossible – and perhaps I can get a group of friends together for a lovely week at an AirBnB to start with!

14

Calling Dr. Beat

Music is one of the most reliable ways to boost your mood and adjust your attitude. There's lots of research proving that music not only reduces anxiety and depression, but it stimulates the brain's reward centres and gives us instant feelings of happiness. Listening to music can lower blood pressure, improve memory, and even reduce physical pain.

Most of us listen to music that makes us feel happily nostalgic about simpler times, such as anthems from high school or songs our parents played when we were children. Imagine if you had all of these songs in one playlist for a mega mood boost?

This list will help you have some musical medicine on hand for when you're in need of a brighter outlook.

Make a list of ten tracks that never fail to boost your mood.

Your entries can include guilty pleasures, songs that conjure up good memories, and tried and true feel-good anthems.

Songs that I know will put me in a good mood are rarely the kind of stuff I studied for my music degree. I tend to go for pop, and lately I've been listening to the past 20 years of Eurovision entries. Maybe there should be a study about musical taste level dropping as happiness levels increase!

You'll already know your favourite mood-boosting bops, and the trick here is to put them all in one place.

 **TAKE ACTION**

You can listen to your playlist by yourself, or invite a friend/family member over and share your favourite uplifting songs. Have fun with this! Feel free to blast the music, sing into your hairbrush and dance around your living room.

A great time to schedule a listening session is when you know you'll need a boost, perhaps to overcome a case of the Mondays or if you know you'll be stuck in traffic on your commute home.

If I feel like I'm in a bit of a rut, putting on one of my joyful playlists always helps me feel lighter, more optimistic and ready to enjoy my day. Within an instant I've forgotten my bad mood, and I'm lip-syncing with a big smile on my face.

15

Healthy habits

Acknowledging your good and bad habits in list form lets you see them from a different perspective. It will help you make a plan to add items to the good column and cross off some bad habits. These small, incremental changes will improve your quality of life, and help your mind, body and heart function better for your optimum happiness!

Make a list of all of your healthy habits, and another list of your bad habits.

Include your usual hygiene routines, self-care, exercise, nutrition, emotions – anything you do for yourself that adds to your 'health bank'. Similarly, list any habits you have that take away from the health bank.

There's always a trade-off with bad habits, that's why they're considered 'bad'. For instance, working through lunch and not eating during your lunch break will likely result in low energy and afternoon brain fog.

Likewise, have a think about the trade-off of your good habits. Yes, exercising regularly is time-consuming, but it makes you feel great, helps you manage stress and increases lifespan. Totally worth it!

TAKE ACTION

Choose three good habits that you could add into your life, do more frequently or upgrade to the next level, and add them to your calendar for the month.

What can you clean up? Are there any that stick out to you that cause you more stress than they're worth?

Choose three bad habits you'd like to vanquish first, and make a plan for the next month of how you'll change your ways.

You could take on your bad habit of working through lunch by making plans with a co-worker or friend to eat lunch together for some magical accountability.

One of my favourite good habits is planning meals for the week. I love being able to see yummy food and good nutrition laid out for my future. From my plan, I can make a shopping list and buy in everything I need for the week. When I don't plan in advance, while it's not the end of the world, my meals are either very boring or unhealthy and overly calorific. A bad habit would be when I give in to my laziness or overwhelm after a busy day and I don't want to cook dinner, so I just order takeaway. This isn't always aligned with my healthy nutrition goals.

Making a plan helps combat decision fatigue, leaving energy for the more important decisions I need to make for my life, health and business. I've learned it's well worth it to make a plan!

16

Forgiveness list

We all carry around old emotional baggage from the past, and without knowing it, its heaviness shapes our decisions and outlook on different situations. This forgiveness list is inspired by Ho'oponopono, the traditional Hawaiian practice of reconciliation and forgiveness. It's a list I make regularly, and I focus on different areas of my life (especially if I'm experiencing a 'roadblock').

Carrying issues from the past and their related negative emotions is like walking around with a pebble in your shoe. It's a low-level pain that we can choose not to live with! Forgiving these past events will offload them from your mind and heart, and make you more positive and open to new experiences.

List out the first ten negative memories from your life associated with this category on a scrap piece of paper.

You can pick a category: family, relationships, friendships, money, work, etc. If you're stuck, start chronologically with your earliest memories and go up through your timeline. You want to identify any moments of your life that pop up in your head and cause any negative self-talk, shame or guilt.

I've been making this list regularly for about five years now, so I struggled coming up with an example for this book (which is great). I chose the 'work' category and remembered a time from my old career when I lost my cool in a meeting during some management changes. I was a bit embarrassed about it afterwards, and I kind of shocked myself. I definitely don't want to carry this memory around, so this is something I need to release and forgive myself of!

 **TAKE ACTION**

Set aside an hour to complete this task in the next month.

One by one, address each memory by feeling the associated emotions, mentally forgive the memories, person or situation and say goodbye. Often you'll find you'll be forgiving yourself! You can burn the paper afterwards, if you like a ritual. Keep doing this for different areas of your life and you'll find your lists get shorter over time, and you'll feel an overall sense of peace.

This task isn't easy at first, but the lightness you'll enjoy afterwards is long-lasting and you'll find yourself navigating life with a lot less stress. Let it go!

17

The A-team

Studies have shown that surrounding ourselves with positive, happy people has been proven to increase our happiness. This is because we tend to copy the behaviours and attitudes of those around us, so it's really important to make sure you've got some of those rays of sunshine in your life.

These people are the best ones to get involved on your happiness practice journey, they will make it a lot lighter and more fun, and give you a better chance of reaching your highest life satisfaction.

Getting these bright buddies involved with your list-making will benefit all of you. Research has proven that we are more successful at reaching our goals when we collaborate and team up with others who have similar aims. When you strive for goals together as a group, this social context greatly increases your chances of success.

This list is set up to help you identify the people in your life whose glass is half full, to join you on your *List Yourself Happy* adventures.

Make a list of between two and five people you trust who are generally positive and would like to join you in making lists for happiness.

You can involve family members, dear friends, colleagues or your partner. I have found making lists with others can be life-affirming and very fun.

I dedicate this list to my best pal Jim who has been making lists with me since I was an awkward teenager. We wrote down our dreams, hopes and creative conquests, learning so much about each other in the process. This is probably why we have such a strong bond to this day. I wish this for you and your friends.

 **TAKE ACTION**

Start a list-making group to work on the lists from this book.

Invite these lovely people to join you in your regular happiness practice, and let the joy abound! You can collaborate with this group on a monthly basis and call it a List Club. Following each other's successes and sharing your ideas from the lists will provide insight to each other's true selves, and make you all feel a strong sense of connection.

Having a monthly meet-up will also provide accountability to make sure you do the work in the lists. Like a board meeting for your life enjoyment!

18

Foods that bring you joy

Specific foods can conjure up warm memories from childhood, special events and travel. Eating, cooking and baking are great ways to connect with your soul, to care for yourself and others, and to find comfort.

Certain foods will feel like 'treats', which you can indulge in luxuriously. Having treats to look forward to makes life much more exciting! This list needn't all be treat-focused, because you surely love a wide array of foods – summer strawberries, or rich-scented sun-ripened tomatoes, for instance. Knowing what you like will tell you more about how to look after yourself in a nourishing way.

Make a list of all of the delicious foods that make you happy.

Your list can include nostalgic foods from childhood, things you crave often, a certain item from a local bakery that blows your mind or meaningful, ceremonial treats like birthday cake or your favourite type of Christmas cookies.

Growing up, I learned how to cook from my mother and grandmother who were both very seasonal cooks. We fully celebrated all the special occasions throughout the year by making menus and recipes according to our traditions and the seasonal produce available.

As an adult, I find so much happiness and comfort in carrying on this seasonal celebratory approach to food, and cooking gives me such peace. Not everything on my list is home-cooked – I get a lot of joy from Twiglets, tahini, potatoes, pizza, crumpets, Sunday roasts (I'm almost British by now!), strawberries, and my local Indian, Ethiopian and Turkish restaurants. My list is ever-evolving as I try new things – food is such an exciting adventure for me.

TAKE ACTION

Take a look at your list, and make a plan to eat at least one of these delicious foods in the next month.

If you plan to cook something, buy the ingredients and set a date to make the dish. If you'd like to visit a café, bakery or restaurant, invite your friends or take your partner on a date. If some items on your list are seasonal, you can plan further into the year and set yourself a reminder to eat, cook and bake your way to happiness!

I have tahini saved on my online grocery shop's 'favourites' list, and it is automatically added to my order so I never have to live without it.

For years I've created menus for every holiday, celebration and dinner party, and I save them in a folder in my Google Drive. Feel free to embrace technology here, unless you prefer to use an old-school recipe box. That's cute, too.

19

It's the little things

While sometimes 'little things' may feel trivial compared to the larger issues going on in the world, it's important to give yourself regular joy injections!

This list will help you identify the smaller things in life that light you up, and encourage you to enjoy them more often or more intensely. Even if you can't recreate some of the items on this list, you might find that just thinking about them will put a smile on your face.

Make a list of ten smaller, silly, tiny things that bring you joy.

Your list can include anything small, from sipping your favourite tea or wearing an item of clothing you love to having a staring contest with your cat. It can be watching videos from your favourite comedian, or hearing the relaxing sound of a train in the distance. Your entries should be all about what's truly joyful for you, no matter how silly or how inconsequential they might seem to others.

I love making this list because I try to fill my life with these tiny joys, and it's such a wonderful thing to think about. I love the inkiness of a Pilot V7 pen on sketchbook paper. The sigh my dog Marlowe makes when he settles into his bed for the night. Taking a bath before bed and sleeping in freshly washed sheets. Listening to an 80s-themed internet radio station and Anita Baker comes on. Seeing someone trip on an uneven pavement and try to style it out. Haha!

TAKE ACTION

Select the items from your list that you can bring into your life more regularly, and make a plan to do or reenact one item every week for the next month.

You could make sure your favourite shirt is ready to wear regularly, or buy variations of it so you can make it part of your look. You could have staring contests with your cat every afternoon as you sip your favourite tea.

For instance, I should keep my sketchbook and V7 pen at the ready so I can indulge in more writing, drawing and list-making. Perhaps I should record Marlowe's bedtime sigh to my phone, to enjoy on tap and for posterity. I could work the bath/clean sheets thing into my weekly self-care ritual, and listen to Anita Baker's back catalogue on Spotify. I'm sure there are countless blooper videos on YouTube of people tripping on the pavement to watch!

The point here is to make sure these things happen in your day for an injection of joy. You can even build your day around them, for maximum lightness and fulfilment!

20

Fake a smile

This is the one time when being fake actually benefits you!
You can trick your mind into happiness by simply smiling.

I love that whenever I see research about smiling it automatically
makes the corners of my mouth turn up. It's the same as when
someone writes 'take a deep breath' and I do just that as a
reflex. Our minds and our bodies react really well to these cues,
and I believe it's one of the most interesting and beautiful parts
of being human.

Research has proven that putting a self-imposed smile on your
face when you're feeling down boosts your mood. A 2008 study
published in the *Journal of Pain* found that just by expressing an
emotion, you can make yourself feel that very emotion. I guess
now we know what all these actors are going through while
they're method acting their way through hilarious comedies
and, yikes, the darker stories. Hats off to them.

One study that makes me chuckle is from the University of Cardiff
in Wales, which found that people who could not frown due to
botox injections were happier than those who could physically
frown. This is the first bit of research that might make me actually
consider such enhancement. It gives some truth to 'fake it 'til you
make it'.

Research also shows that smiling helps reduce stress and lowers
our heart rates in tense situations. This list will help you smile
more so you can bask in all of these benefits.

Create a list of things that are guaranteed to make you smile.

Your entries can include something funny, beautiful, heartwarming, cute or hopeful. Even looking at random photos on the internet of other people smiling can make your corners turn up – just try to fight it!

Turn that frown upside down! It takes more muscles to frown than it does to smile, so focus on being the personal trainer of your grin.

Animals are a great source of smiles. My husband Charles loves seeing the smile of our dog Marlowe when he's happily bathing in the grass. He is always watching videos of the baby elephants of Kenya's Sheldrick Wildlife Trust on Instagram. I just told him I was mentioning these in my book and he smiled BIG.

See, just talking about smiling brings smiles to our faces!

One sure-fire way for me to smile is by going through old photos on my laptop. There are some hilarious moments from our events, fun times with my friends and wonderful awkward moments that just bring me joy. I've tried editing my photos in public at cafés or shared workspaces, and I've been a bit worried about how elated I look to innocent passersby. Luckily, I know that my beaming face only inspires more happiness and I shouldn't feel worried at all.

TAKE ACTION

This month, surround yourself by these smile triggers, and smile more than you ever have before.

Build these smile-inducing moments into habits for your every day. One way to engineer this is by following your smiles as they come, and build on them.

If you have a certain friend that always cracks you up, spend more time with them. If you love the silliness of a certain TV show or YouTube channel, set them as one of the pages that automatically opens up on your laptop, app or tablet.

You could unfollow all those people on Insta that make you feel lesser, and replace them with the most adorable animals instead. You could add a bookmark folder to your web browser and collect online pages, channels, photos and videos, and simply name it 'Smile'.

Don't forget, smiles are contagious. Don't be surprised if you suddenly feel like you're living a Broadway version of your life! As Louis Armstrong sang back in 1928, 'When you're smiling, the whole world smiles with you'.

21

Meditation is mandatory

I repeat, meditation is mandatory. There are lots of reasons why I'm telling you this, the necessity and benefits of meditation are rooted in science, and regular meditation as a practice has been carried through all world religions since the beginning of humankind.

The main reason the big M is being mentioned in this book is because I am living proof that it directly affects my own personal happiness, relaxation and life enjoyment. If you asked me which of my lists would have the biggest effect on your mental health and happiness, this would be it. Meditation is the foundation of mindfulness and mood regulation. It stops anxiety in its tracks. It simply makes me a better person and I have way more fun when I meditate daily.

I've been meditating since my mom taught me and my siblings when we were little. We'd sit in the backyard on the grass, cross-legged, backs straight, and meditate to the sound of the breeze through the trees. I went on to use meditation to prime my mind before games and competitions when I played sports, did theatre and sang in school concerts, and before I went on stage as the lead singer of a jazz orchestra in university. It helped me overcome panic attacks when I graduated university with a music degree and had no idea what to do next!

There have been periods of time when I've fallen out of practice, and life is just not as good when I'm not centred.

I still meditate every day, and before every performance and appearance. I calm myself, set an intention, breathe, and let my body and mind balance out so I can do my very best. Okay, now you know my secret!

Make a list of three ways you'd like to try meditation, or raise your meditation practice to a new level.

If this is totally new to you, you may need to do a bit of research on how people usually meditate, so you can decide what sounds most comfortable to you.

Beginners normally benefit from a guided meditation, where someone talks you through visualizations or suggests some mantras. More experienced meditators can just sit still, focus on their breathing and relax. Thoughts will come up for everyone, this is totally natural. You just have to shoo them away and get back to relaxing. It definitely gets easier and more blissful the more you practise.

If you're already an expert meditator, hooray! Perhaps it's time to try a new form of meditation, like a flame meditation, or you could add in more regular sessions to your practice. Mix it up!

TAKE ACTION

Schedule in half an hour per week this month to try meditation, or elevate/increase your practice.

Set aside time in your calendar for this, and prepare a space where you can sit down and breathe. You'll probably want to close the door to the room and make sure you're warm enough. You can simply meditate like this, by focusing on the rhythm of your breath and try to completely relax your body and mind.

Meditation is free, you don't need any props or equipment, so there aren't any relevant excuses to avoid it. If you feel like half an hour is too much at first, then just try ten minutes. It will get easier as you go, and it's almost addictive once you start feeling so good from it!

Whenever I meditate around my dog, he falls asleep and breathes so deeply. I think maybe calmness is contagious. I find his breathing so comforting and relaxing, and I refer to these sessions as 'Marlowe meditations'. My favourite kind.

22

Ten movies you'd watch repeatedly

Rewatching your favourite movies brings a sense of nostalgia, whether it be about childhood or simpler times, or perhaps you first watched the movie with someone important to you. Perhaps certain stories from the movies really resonate with you and your values, so it's enjoyable to revisit their messages.

Having a quiet night in to savour your favourite cinematic worlds and stories is such a wonderful way to relax and enjoy your space.

Make a list of ten movies you'd watch over and over again.

My movie list for this is way more than ten, because I'm a very nostalgic person and I use movies as part of my seasonal theming. I'm amazed by the creation process of a movie, so even if I don't like the movie, I truly respect all the work that's gone into it.

I believe *Pee-Wee's Big Adventure* helped shape me as a light-hearted creative, and I watch it to recharge my positive outlook. Every autumn I watch the entire *Harry Potter* catalogue – I feel nostalgic for Hogwarts even though I was never enrolled there. Charles and I watch the dystopian *V for Vendetta* every 5th November, originally to stay mindful of how democracy can crumble, and in more recent years to find catharsis – 'at least it's not as bad as this'. I watch *The Hunger Games* trilogy for the same reason.

And then there are all the glorious seasonal movies such as *Hocus Pocus* at Halloween, and *National Lampoon's Christmas Vacation*, *Elf* and *Die Hard*, which are on heavy rotation in our house in December.

 **T A K E   A C T I O N**

From your list, figure out which movies you do not already own and buy one in the next month, so you have them ready for uplifting (or cathartic) viewing.

I still have the original DVDs of some of the movies I mentioned, and the rest have been purchased or added to a list ready for me to watch on a streaming service. Schedule in time for yourself to relax and enjoy these movies, and maybe even plan a 'watch party' with your friends. How about starting a Top Ten Film Club and take turns hosting?

23

Random acts of kindness

We've all heard of the concept of performing 'random acts of kindness', but it's the sort of thing that we tend to forget to actually do. Showing kindness and going out of your way to do caring, helpful things for others has been proven to increase happiness levels in both the giver and receiver. Everyday life and responsibilities can so easily make us self-focused, and we forget that doing a good deed will make us feel fantastic.

Make a list of random acts of kindness you'd like to perform for your friends, family, community, strangers, the world!

While planning ahead makes the acts less 'random' to you, it will still be random to the recipient.

A great way to approach this task is by utilizing your strengths and privilege. For instance, you could go out of your way to email feedback to a company when you've had a positive experience with one of their employees. You could buy a coffee for the person in line behind you – or for everyone in line! Simply paying a compliment to someone is a great place to start.

TAKE ACTION

Make time in your schedule to carry out an idea from your list at least once a week during the next month, and prepare to bask in that warm fuzzy feeling.

Get ready to feel a mega mood-boost as you bring joy and thoughtfulness to others! Choose four items from your list and make them happen. Kindness can be addictive, so soon you may find yourself putting all the items from your list into action and having to come up with more ideas.

I love the infinity aspect of this practice – you're giving your kindness to the world, which makes you happier and thus more likely to give kindness to the world...

The benefits of this rely on the action, so you've got to make sure you can remember to carry out the kindness. I have a habit of putting sticky notes on the back of my front door with mantras, intentions, attitude adjustments, so when I leave the house I am positive and open-hearted. Sometimes I add a random act of kindness reminder there, or schedule them into my calendar so I get a notification on my phone.

I find it's helpful to have an elf-like mindset here, an almost mischievous feeling as you come up with ways to brighten someone's day. It's kind of like pranking, but doing helpful, thoughtful things for others.

24

Things I want to learn

One of the secrets to feeling energized and optimistic is to maintain a growth mindset. Learning is *fun*-damental, and if you dedicate your life to exploring and improving you will never get bored. Often we give up on learning new things because we assume we know what we're good at, bad at, and that's it. You stick to what you know, and that gets monotonous.

The act of learning has been proven to help relieve anxiety and depression, and gives us an overall sense of wellbeing. If you ever feel like you're living in Groundhog Day, the perfect antidote is to get curious and bring some new skills, information and knowledge into that beautiful brain of yours. The added bonus is you'll stay sharp, witty and interesting well into your twilight years!

Make a list of all the things you'd like to learn.

This can include new skills for your professional, personal or fitness interests, subjects you'd like to explore out of sheer curiosity or solutions to things you encounter everyday. Whatever you write down, make sure it sounds fun to you – this list isn't about getting a raise or better productivity, unless you find that fun.

You could deep-dive and study all of Beethoven's symphonies, research how to take better care of your houseplants or look up instructional crochet videos.

My list often includes things I want to cook, dress patterns to make, and video editing to master. I've been trying to learn to do the splits since I was a kid, so this often ends up on my to-learn list. Maybe this year!

 **T A K E   A C T I O N**

Choose the item on your list that looks the most fun or interesting, and allocate one hour per week in your calendar this month to devote to learning more about it.

With so much information now readily available at our fingertips, these days we don't really have any excuse for not learning new things.

Focusing on one thing from your list this month will help you to really enjoy exploring it, plus you'll have substantial knowledge to show for it!

For my project of learning the splits, I know this will take regular practice and lots of stretching, so even if I don't reach my goal I will certainly be more flexible than when I started! For the video editing, I could spend an hour watching how-to videos on YouTube and get some practice by editing a video of my dog.

25

Totes emosh playlist

In modern society, we're often discouraged from showing our feelings, and 'a stiff upper lip' is rewarded as an act of bravery. The fact is, most of us aren't allowing ourselves to process our feelings in a healthy way. Feelings that are swept under the rug always come out eventually and in some form, often in ways that don't reflect your best self.

One way to get your feelings flowing is by listening to music that makes you feel a wide spectrum of emotions. We often use music to uplift and motivate ourselves, such as creating workout playlists, but engaging with music that makes us 'totes emosh' is a valuable tool to embrace feelings we don't always want to face.

A recent study found that listening to sad music is a common activity that's been linked with increased happiness across the world's cultures. It's shown that listening this way helps us regulate our moods and negative emotions. Another study found that music universally evokes thirteen different human emotions, but for this list we're just accessing three: sad, relaxing and beautiful. We're fortunate to live in this modern society that gives us access to a never-ending library of music, online and for free.

Make a list of ten songs that make you feel totally emotional.

I recommend choosing songs that conjure up feelings of sadness, wistfulness, happy nostalgia, relaxation and beauty.

This is not a playlist for break-up songs that make you rage (although it's good to have one of those handy too). What you want to achieve is a release, and to face the emotions that are bubbling up inside you.

On my list is Dolly Parton's original *I Will Always Love You*, which gets me every time, as does *How Far I'll Go* from the *Moana* soundtrack. I tear up just writing about it! I've asked for only ten songs here, but this is only a start, and you should add to this list as you discover songs that give you the feels.

 **TAKE ACTION**

Turn this into a playlist and take a quiet moment this month to listen to it and feel your emotions.

Schedule in some time for yourself to listen to music that moves your emotions and if the moment takes you, feel free to have a good cry session. You'll want to set at least half an hour aside for this, and make sure you'll be undisturbed so you can really let it go. Ensure you have tissues and a glass of water to hand.

Of course, this process really helps when you have things going on in your life that are upsetting, and perhaps you've been pushing your emotions down because you've been putting on a brave face. But it also works well as a release ritual that you can perform whenever you need it, say after a trying work week or when you're feeling generally salty and frustrated.

26

Immediate surroundings

Set up your immediate surroundings so you can boost your mood or change your attitude in a snap. The goal is to look around your place and feel like you have so many options to relax, enjoy and inspire around you.

This list will come to the rescue when you're looking for an instant recharge to get your positivity, creativity and happiness flowing. They're the sort of quick fixes that you know you can rely on to change your outlook on life.

Give yourself the best chance to enjoy your life, maintain a happy mood and feel fulfilled!

Make a list of things that you can make readily available to boost your mood.

Think about how you can get easy access to your mood-boosters without planning, thinking or trying. Consider all the senses, and the types of activities you usually enjoy.

You can light a scented candle, keep your favourite type of bubble bath on display in the bathroom, put an iconic fashion photography book on your coffee table or place your favourite vinyl next to your record player. You could display thank-you notes or cards you've received from loved ones, or a cartoon from *The New Yorker* that always makes you burst out laughing.

I have a wall of photos of people I love in my hallway, they range from family photos from childhood to group photos that were taken at big birthday parties. I look at them every night when I brush my teeth and I'm reminded of how much I'm loved, and what an amazing support system exists around me.

 **TAKE ACTION**

Choose three ideas from your list, and make them easy to access. Use, admire and engage in them regularly for an instant charge of happiness this month.

Buy yourself some beautiful matches to set next to your scented candle. Take a long bath with your favourite bubbles. Leaf through your fashion photography book and bask in the beauty. Lay down and enjoy the crackle of your favourite vinyl.

You most likely have everything on hand already, but you just need to put these things on display and in places that are visible and within easy reach. Since I have the photos readily displayed, I can be reminded of the people I love every day.

Another mood boost for me is having a big bowl of fruit on the kitchen table – it's so colourful and reminds me of how lucky I am to live on our beautiful and bountiful Earth – and putting cinnamon essential oil in a diffuser makes me feel really cosy and looked after.

27

Let's get physical

People are currently living the most sedentary lifestyles in human history. Our physical activity has been slowly declining through the ages. Now that we're in the Big Data Age, with ever-advancing technology and desk-based work (and add Netflix to the mix), we are mostly living a physically lazy day. The effects are pretty grim, including health issues like obesity, diabetes, heart disease and certain cancers. This lack of movement is also directly associated with depression and anxiety, so it's very clear that one should heed the words of Gloria Estefan and *Get On Your Feet*.

It's time to bring back your inner hunter-gatherer, and move that body! We all have our own personal favourite forms of exercise, so making a list of ways that are fun for you to move your body will motivate you to do it regularly.

Make a list of ten fun ways to exercise.

You can include any form of movement, from simply walking in the park to participating in organized sports. Include whatever feels fun or easy. As long as you're moving, you're on the right track!

Most of my exercise requires a spoonful of sugar, such as involving fun music, a destination or friends. One of my favourite ways to exercise is instructor-led spinning with cheesy pop music as, for me, it doesn't even feel like exercise! I love taking long country walks if there's a pub at the end of the route. I will always join my friends in taking music video dance classes.

TAKE ACTION

Plan a few of these different types of exercise into your calendar this month.

If you truthfully listed entries you thought were fun, you should be looking forward to this month! If you feel like it might be a struggle, go back to the drawing board until you've got a collection of activities you can't wait to try.

To give yourself the best chance of success, it's worth considering that some activities might take more organization than others. Do you need to pull together any special kit for mountain biking and set it out in advance? Maybe you need to find your swimming goggles from last summer before your trip to the pool. Prepare whatever you need in advance so you don't wriggle out of it.

It's also important to know and honour your biorhythms and plan accordingly. I would love to be one of those people who run a 10K at the break of dawn but I'm not. I'll do some late-morning yoga on a Saturday or pre-lunch spinning on a weekday. If you're not a morning person, and you're trying to fit in a swim or bike ride on an early weekday morning, you might miss out on your active fun. Plan ahead and give yourself your best chance to move!

28

Sweet dreams

There have been countless studies about sleep and its huge effect on our physical and mental health. The quality of our sleep pretty much affects every area of our lives, and lack of sleep can even be dangerous and decrease life expectancy.

I love technology, I probably have more screens than most people, and my enthusiasm for apps, games and television is pretty robust. But these things directly and negatively affect sleep, and as modern humans we've got to set some boundaries.

In addition to the lull of the blue light, other factors such as eating or exercising late, lack of exercise, or drinking too much coffee can all set us back in our sleep efforts. It may sound like a losing battle, but with a little forward planning and mindfulness, we can nudge ourselves towards the sleep of our... dreams!

List ten ways you can adjust your behaviour, routine or surroundings for better sleep.

Lowering your caffeine intake, making sure you get plenty of exercise, and reading a book for an hour before bedtime are all great ways to help you sleep soundly. Only you know your behaviour and habits, so this list should be highly personalized to make it more actionable.

My sleep patterns can be a bit intermittent at the best of times, and especially if I'm travelling a lot. My active mind is always trying to write emails or social posts in my head, or plan for the future. Zip it, brain! Over the years I've trained to be a sleep athlete, and I'm definitely my best self after 8.5 hours of sleep.

When I don't get the amount of sleep I need, I get hungry at weird times and crave junk food, my mood is low and I avoid exercise. Also, I'm less productive because I feel like I'm walking through fog. Not getting enough sleep is a lose-lose situation.

 **TAKE ACTION**

This month, try to apply all these adjustments and keep a sleep journal to track your hours.

Some of these steps can easily be put in place, such as moving your phone charger out of the bedroom so that you don't scroll before bed. Others will take practice, if you're trying to build a new habit of not eating after 8pm for instance. It may help to tell others in your household that you are making changes to your routines so that you can improve your sleep.

Keeping a sleep journal is useful because you can track how you slept, for how long, how you felt when you woke up, and what factors from the previous day affected your sleep. There are lots of apps for this if you don't want to keep a physical journal. Over time, you can see what behaviours and habits are affecting your sleep and you can tweak them accordingly.

29

Miracle Grow

Sometimes we get stuck in a rut and we feel powerless about living the life we really want. It can all be overwhelming, and there is so much information out there about improving your life that your head spins. The fact is, we have so much control over the lives we lead, and when we focus on a specific area the answers begin to appear clearly.

In order to keep overwhelm at bay, choose what area of your life you would like to evolve and grow. For instance, relationships, health, finances, love, self-care, creativity are all specific enough compartments to get you going.

This list is a bit of magic – focusing on one area helps your mind creatively come up with ways to actually improve. There are lots of terms for this sort of focused thinking, including 'niching' and 'chunking down', but I call it Miracle Grow because it's so surprisingly effective.

Choose a specific area of your life that you'd like to improve, and make a list based on what aspects you'd like to change.

For instance, if you're feeling financially challenged, you'd perhaps write that you'd like to have a certain amount of money in the bank. If you'd like to improve your relationships with others, you could write that you'd like to hear from them more, or get to know them better.

I recently applied this approach to my friendships, as I had become a bit insular and wasn't reaching out and connecting with some of my friends as much as usual. I hadn't really noticed – life just went on and I realized I was starting to feel a bit lonely and adrift. Upon closer inspection, I realized that I just needed to put a bit more effort in and reach out more regularly.

 **T A K E   A C T I O N**

Choose one item from your list, and commit to making it happen this month.

For instance, if you would like to improve your bank balance, you could find ways to bring in more income this month, or ways you could tighten the belt. If you'd like to have a closer relationship with a certain family member, you could call them for a heart-to-heart, or send them a thoughtful gift.

Once I reached out to my friends and made an effort to see them more regularly, not only did I feel so much better, but they did as well. The knock-on effects were plentiful, we ended up feeling more supported, loved and understood.

It's incredible how creative you become when you focus on finding a solution for a problem, or something that needs improving. When sorting out your life seems like an insurmountable task, just choosing one bit to tackle first will give you the confidence to look at the other areas.

30

Thanks, past self!

We may not notice it, but the lives we lead today are a product of how we've set ourselves up to live. We develop good (and bad) habits, mindsets and beliefs as we go, and our actions related to these things create our reality. For example, your healthy teeth and gums are a result of your dedication to daily flossing. Your choice to automatically move part of your salary into savings every month means that you've built up a comforting rainy-day fund. Thanks, past self!

I'm so glad I developed a meditation habit at a young age, because I think it's a big part of why I tend to see the bright side of life. My belief that everyone can achieve their dreams through list-making has been built over years of finding my own successes this way, and seeing it happen for others many times.

Make a list of things you can do today that you'll be thankful for in the future.

These can include anything from starting a new healthy habit, or putting money into an index-tracking fund, to simply ironing all the clothes in your wardrobe. Ooh, that last one made my Virgo heart flutter!

I'd recommend thinking about how you want to feel in the future, and focus on what you can do for yourself now to help that along. Do you want to feel more positive, more financially secure, healthier, more relaxed?

As an over-achiever and an American, I'm not very good at taking breaks. I have to remind myself that it's healthy to block out time to take a break and relax. Thankfully, being immersed in British culture (such experts at holiday-making) I'm reminded that vacations are a thing and that I should take them. Planning breaks in advance is a really good practice that benefits my mental health, the quality of my work and the people in my life.

 **TAKE ACTION**

Choose one item from your list and give your future self this gift in the next month.

Make a start on your beautiful happy future now! If you've chosen a habit, consider that it takes repetition to get it going, so schedule it in or leave reminders for yourself until the habit feels natural. For instance, if I wanted to feel healthier, I might commit to a daily health checklist or use an app to remind me to take vitamins, do exercise, drink eight glasses of water, etc.

If you've chosen a new mindset or attitude, start building towards this by scheduling in activities that support it. You could set daily pop-up reminders on your phone, such as 'I love my life!'. Dedicating time towards maintaining a positive attitude will give you a 100% chance of success. It's like magic. The important thing here is to actually take the step. It might be tempting to do the research about the thing, or maybe journal about it, but this list is all about taking actions that truly benefit your future self.

31

Hobbies

Having hobbies is a wonderful way to layer more joy into our lives, and to engage in the playfulness we experienced during childhood. Hobbies can allow us to express our creativity, to connect with others and to enjoy a feeling of peaceful flow.

Too often we prioritize chores, or unnecessarily stay late at work, or our go-to way to relax is to binge-watch TV shows on the sofa. Before you know it you can't even remember what you did yesterday, let alone if you enjoyed it. Research shows that we get the most life-satisfaction and happiness through experiences, especially when they are shared with others.

Make a list of hobbies you'd love to add to your life.

These can be creative outlets such as woodworking, painting, gardening, or focused pastimes like birdwatching or stamp collecting. Don't forget to list the hobbies that you've already taken up, but would like to spend more time doing. If you feel yourself veering into productive mode when coming up with these list items, keep reminding yourself that it's supposed to be fun. The theme here is 'play'!

I dip in and out of my favourite hobbies. It's so easy to forget to enjoy yourself for your own sake, and I know I've neglected to engage in this playfulness when I feel bored. By the way, I truly believe the sentiment of boredom is self-inflicted and unnecessary. It's preposterous to feel bored when you have constant access to your brain and imagination. I've always delighted in how the French say 'to be bored' – the verb is *s'ennuyer*, which translates as 'to bore one's self'. Accurate!

TAKE ACTION

Choose one item from your list and plan in one hour in the next month to learn about and immerse yourself in this hobby.

Enjoy yourself with this hobby and feel free to spend more than one hour on it this month if you can! One way to get started is by signing up for a course online or in person, learning more about it and actually doing the thing. Or you can just get stuck in by gathering together all the supplies you need and going for it.

It's really important to carve out time for sheer enjoyment. I want you to be feeling so free and joyful it's like you're a kid again. You deserve this level of bliss! When I'm engaging in one of my hobbies, I know I'm in that happy state of flow because I realize I'm actually smiling.

There's been growing enthusiasm for bird watching over the past few years, and I'm tempted to join in the fun because they're beautiful creatures, I'd be spending time in nature and the gamer in me would want to 'collect' as many species as I can. Yes, I know that's a nerdy sentence, but one of the best things about hobbies is you get to embrace your inner geek!

32

You've made it!

We all have different perspectives on what success looks like, and these ideas mostly come from cultural influences such as movies we've seen, celebrities, successful people we follow, or perhaps adults we looked up to during childhood.

Your unique design of success is important because you may find that most of your entries are achievable now, or in the near future. Also, it's important to set big lofty goals because they tell us more about our personal style of success.

What does 'making it' mean to you?

Your list doesn't have to include physical things – you can describe a feeling, or add support services (like a housekeeper) to your entries.

Will you have the Porsche, a private island, a wine fridge? As a child of the 80s, I grew up watching films steeped in conspicuous consumption and excess. Most examples of success were played by men in fancy three-piece suits. My personal framing of 'making it' defaults to be quite cheesy as a result, and I've had to make this list many times to get to the bottom of what I really want.

I'll know I've 'made it' when I have the house of my dreams, the perfect setting for parties and celebrations with my loved ones. Yes, I still want a red Porsche, but the thought of having lots of space for sleepovers with my friends and family makes me giddy.

There is also an unusual number of suits in my wardrobe for someone who is famously known for wearing sequins. Hmm...

 **TAKE ACTION**

Take one item from your list and attempt to achieve it (or at least 'try it on') in the next month.

Okay, perhaps if you've chosen to attempt the dream car, it might be out of reach right now. But you could schedule in a test drive or simply visit the showroom and put yourself in the situation as if you're ready to buy. Would you behave differently if you'd already 'made it'?

Exposure to the experience will make it easier to achieve. In some cases, you might find the thing you were after is not 'all that' after all.

33

Curate your messaging

Whether we notice it or not, we are constantly receiving messages from other people, corporations, news outlets, society and social media. We tend to be products of our surroundings, and if you're constantly bombarded by false images of perfection, clickbait advertising and negative news stories, it can be hard to stay positive.

But I have great news! You can actively curate what messaging comes into your world by doing a bit of decluttering and adding more positive sources of information to your everyday.

Make a list of ways to bring more positive messaging and inspiring information into your environment.

You can seek out influences that help give you a better sense of belonging, set yourself some uplifting reminders and follow social media accounts that are filled with the sentiment that you are okay and totally enough.

I'd like you to focus on seeking sources that make you feel happy as you are, so please try to stay away from any messaging that makes you feel like you need to lose a stone in weight, or start a six-figure business, or be like certain celebrities.

TAKE ACTION

Spend one hour a week this month decluttering any feeds, emails, chat groups, apps, etc. from your life, and replace them with more positive uplifting versions from your list.

You really won't miss the negative stuff. If you really miss reading the news you can seek it out, but unless you work in an industry that requires it, you should turn off breaking news notifications because it's rarely good news! Also, don't forget to edit out the 'time-wasters': distracting, superfluous updates and messages that come into your life. This is the stuff that you either have to mark as read, or you feel guilty for ignoring them (hello, random WhatsApp chat group), or Instagram accounts that aren't relevant to you anymore, etc.

I love to add mood-lifting reminders to my phone that pop up throughout the day, such as snappy messages like mantras or inspiring quotes from my favourite authors to reset my thinking to be more positive. I unsubscribe from newsletters that don't bring me joy, or simply clutter my inbox, and instead subscribe to the ones for things I enjoy or care about. I try to follow uplifting, funny accounts on social media – you can never go wrong with animal memes!

34

A pat on the back

Life can be a very busy affair, and our biggest moments can pass by in a flash. We seldom take enough time to celebrate all we've achieved, and our brain loves to move on to the next goal. Society and exposure to social media can condition us to be in a perpetually wanting state of mind, but we should savour and celebrate all our fantastic achievements.

Taking account of all your accomplishments is something you'd probably never do unless you were directed, which is why I've added this list to your happiness practice. Simply making the first list will have you beaming with pride, and completing the action step will open up doors that will benefit your life for years to come.

Make a list of your proudest achievements.

These can include education, awards and accolades, completing marathons or 5Ks, getting a promotion, having children, starting a business or even your exquisite breakdancing at last year's staff Christmas party. You could add moments when you've asserted boundaries, made lifestyle changes or made new friends.

If we take the time to think of all the amazing things we've achieved, we appreciate and enjoy them and can more readily use them to our advantage. When you consider how hard you worked for something, you'll realize just how good you are at reaching your goals. This self-induced confidence will buoy you more than any outside encouragement.

I'm so proud that I managed to graduate university with a double degree in French with a focus on business, and in Music with a speciality in jazz and composition. I'm also very chuffed that I've completed every Legend of Zelda and Super Mario Bros. game in existence. Winning!

When you're mindful of how far you've come, these accolades act as a foundation to reach even bigger goals, and help you feel more open to connecting with like-minded people and new opportunities.

 **TAKE ACTION**

Choose one of these achievements and do something this month to utilize it, share it, celebrate it, dine out on it! Bask in the glory of your resilience and power.

You could post a photo of the day of your university graduation on social media. You could get a manicure to celebrate that you no longer bite your nails. You could run reports for your business since you started it and marvel at how much it's grown, and share the numbers with your team. Reflection on your successes helps breed motivation to achieve new ones.

Feeling sheepish? If no one knows what you're good at, or how determined you are, or how hard you worked for something, you're shielding a big part of who you are and your values from the world. Don't forget how many people you'll inspire by sharing your story!

35

What makes you unique and wonderful?

Knowing your personal strengths and unique qualities is essential to your happiness practice, because the more you express these features, the more you live truthfully. Too often we try to fit in with the status quo, uncomfortably acting as we think we should act, saying what we think we should say. We end up squelching our feelings, our self-expression, our creativity.

Some of this behaviour is simply primal – early humans survived by living in groups and if you were cast out, your chances of survival on your own were slim and you'd likely be gobbled up by a sabre-toothed tiger. In a way, this type of situation still carries on, where the survival of our mental health depends on human connection. Expressing your uniqueness is important for the soul, but also when you're sharing your true self with the world, it enables you to make the realest of connections.

What makes you unique and wonderful?

Make a list of all of the qualities and tendencies that make you uniquely who you are.

You can include aspects of yourself that you feel you were born with, things that have been conditioned through your experiences, or features that have grown through your creative pursuits and curiosity. Perhaps you're very good at cheering up your friends, or you have a special knack for interior design, or you find epic bliss when dancing (ballet, macarena or otherwise).

For instance, my love of organizing and list-making is evident in so many areas of my life. It's how I am able to keep my business running with a small team, and how I am able to be caring and generous by planning celebrations for my loved ones. My perpetual study of music enables me to sing all the words to a Cardi B song, delight in Bach's Goldberg Variations and wonder at the majestic talents of Nusrat Fateh Ali Khan.

 **TAKE ACTION**

Choose one item from your list and find ways to express it and weave it into your life this month.

Don't worry if you feel that any entries on your list are weird – now's your chance to fly your freak flag! Share who you really are with the world, and get into a practice of doing this. You'll be surprised how much freer you feel by living and celebrating your truths, and you'll deeply connect with others in a way you couldn't have when you had your game face on.

If everyone expressed their uniqueness with the world, it would be a much more colourful and interesting place, and we'd understand each other better.

36

Organized fun

With our busy lives and many responsibilities, it's so easy to find our days filled up with work, chores, commutes and mundane tasks. Our nature tends to lead us towards a work-and-reward mindset, but we often forget to honour the reward part!

We struggle in allowing ourselves to engage in activities that aren't productive to our professional life or running of a household. This list provides you with the gift of forward fun planning, and the action step should be brought into regular practice for optimal happiness.

Make a list of activities that make you feel light, laugh and have fun.

Your entries can range from simple accessible sources of fun such as watching a comedy movie, or skipping across the street instead of walking, to the more involved, such as visiting an amusement park and going on all the rides, or taking in some musical theatre.

Think of ways you can have fun with friends and loved ones, but also by yourself. You'll want to have plenty of ideas on hand, and this list will grow over time as you discover and define all the ways you can amuse yourself!

Making an accessible list of ways to have fun will help you remember to enjoy your life!

TAKE ACTION

Choose four of the items from your list and schedule one in for each week this month.

I recommend mixing simple ideas in with one that takes a bit more planning, so it feels like your life is generously salt and peppered with fun. If you start getting creeping feelings that planning fun in advance is not a valuable use of your time, cast them out immediately. It's these sorts of feelings that made you prioritize chores in the first place and directly affect your happiness hygiene.

It would be great if we didn't have to be so vigilant about having fun, but most of us tend to get in our own way when it comes to engaging in some playtime. Planning in advance ensures any taskmaster tendencies don't intervene! Over time, you will become an expert at filling your life with lightness.

I love to book concerts and experiences in advance, as doing this gives me lots to look forward to and makes my life feel more exciting. I'm always scheduling in wine tastings and drag shows with friends, and if I don't get a monthly karaoke session in the diary, my world turns grey. Planning to meet up with a friend at my local basketball court for an easy game of Horse is always a week-brightener.

37

Build your ideal day

This is a two-part list that will help you take a good look at how you spend your time versus how you wish you *could* spend it. This aerial view can be a wake-up call, and you may be shocked by how much time you spend doing things like scrolling through social media or watching TV. With a bit of clarity, you can more easily hone your days to better match your priorities and values, and maybe even get a bit more rest!

1: List out what you do with your time every day. You can block it out by hours, but keep it in order from when you wake up to when you go to sleep.

You can record your activities throughout an actual day as you live it, from waking up until bedtime. Try to notice how you feel throughout each chunk of time or activity. The next day, assess how you spent your time, and if you used it wisely. Consider the reality of how your day went, and if the way you spent it helped you towards life satisfaction, happiness or reaching your goals.

2: Design your ideal day by making a list of all the activities and meaningful moments you want to happen in your daily life.

Map out how you would love to spend your day, in the same format as List 1. Perhaps it would start with an hour in bed with coffee and listening to music, followed by exercise and a shower, and a morning full of productive, exciting work.

It helps to consider how you'd like to feel throughout the day, and especially at the end of it.

Compare the two lists, assess how they are different, and you will likely find you wouldn't mind swapping one chunk of time from List 1 and replace it with one from List 2.

 **T A K E   A C T I O N**

Schedule in one day this month to stick to your plan for your ideal day, or to permanently replace time blocks from your current days with things from your ideal day.

With this exercise, you can incrementally add more activities and relaxation time as you go, until you are actually living your ideal life! Yes, it will take time and practice to really hone your ideal day but the care and attention to how you spend your time is totally worth it.

38

Sparkle your home for happiness

Keeping a clean and tidy home has very positive effects on our mental health, not to mention it vanquishes harmful germs and dust that can make us ill, or even experience chronic health issues such as asthma.

More worryingly, not staying on top of cleanliness and home hygiene can be one of the signs of depression. The *Personality and Social Psychology Bulletin* published a study reporting that subjects who described their homes as messy experienced more depressive symptoms than those who considered their homes clean and organized.

It's time to let the light in and help your life shine!

List out the regular tasks you need to stay on top of in order to feel like you have your life together and a clean, organized home.

Everyone has a different take on the areas of the home that are most important. For me, it's clean windows, fresh sheets, sparkling countertops and disinfected sinks.

Cleanliness is next to godliness. The state of our surroundings reflects the state of our brains. The peaceful energy of a clean home can make us more productive, reduce stress and allow for better life satisfaction. Putting my home back together and cleaning it thoroughly is one of my favourite ways to stay calm.

TAKE ACTION

This plan could very well become your monthly housekeeping routine that you stick to throughout the year, and having this in place helps you delegate some tasks to others in your household.

You'll want to consider the time of day for certain tasks, for instance, cleaning windows while it's daylight will yield better results than at nighttime.

You could hire a cleaner to do all of this for you, and although we have one come in every other week, I find the act of doing it myself on the off-week is very therapeutic. We put on music and do deeper cleans on areas that maybe our cleaner didn't cover. Our preferred music for cleaning is an internet radio station called Lite 80s, something about singing along with Chaka Khan and Michael McDonald makes us very productive and we actually enjoy doing these chores.

When we're done, I light candles, pour us some delicious drinks and we just sit up and take in the beauty of our home.

39

Perpetual tasks

It's easy to get bogged down by repetitive everyday tasks, and sometimes it can feel like our days are a flurry of chores and menial admin.

Enter the 'Perpetual List'. I learned this trick from my sister Karen (I call her Kiki), who is a busy entrepreneur, a mother of two and a master organizer. She creates 'Perpetual Lists' for various tasks, so that she doesn't have to waste valuable time and energy starting from scratch and making new lists on a regular basis.

Kiki uses this hack in many areas of her life, such as in her business, running her household and for food shopping. Her shopping list in particular is rather epic – she has all the grocery items that she regularly uses listed and laid out by department. Majestic!

Take comfort that such tasks in life are boring and predictable. Since we know they're coming we can plan to better manage them and free up our time for having fun.

Make a list of repetitive tasks and activities you find yourself having to do all the time.

Mentally go through the past week, and think of all the various chores, tasks and admin activities you completed that you don't particularly enjoy. For instance, you may have felt you were constantly doing laundry, or engaged in a pointless work-related email volley that went on and on. A common entry for this list is always 'dishes', and while we can never overcome the battle of dirty dishes, I have helpful advice in the action plan section below.

TAKE ACTION

Assess your perpetual tasks and choose one to tackle by automating, delegating, bundling or adding joyfulness this month.

Automation of mundane tasks is by far my favourite method of freeing up time, and while it can be applied to programming a coffee maker, creating a standing order for your groceries, or setting up canned email responses, it certainly can't be applied to everything. My second favourite is delegation – leaning on others or hiring in help will completely take the task off your plate.

For tasks that can't be automated or delegated, I try to bundle annoying tasks together, so at least they're completed during a set chunk of time. I'll put on some fun music and do the dishes, run the washing machine, dust and vacuum the house in a half-hour chore blitz.

With a creative and open-minded approach, you can hack these tasks to be easier and more fun, or take them off your to-do list once and for all. What will you do with all your extra free time?!

40

Tracking progress

When we focus and track our progress in a specific area of our life, the attention we dedicate to improving gives us much better chances of reaching our goals. The act of tracking progress can be used for so many applications, such as growing a social media following, saving money, and even non-numeric goals such as having more fun!

Make a list of the specific aspects of your life that you'd like to improve, and set deadline dates for when you'd like to reach a certain goal or level of improvement.

For instance, if you'd like to save money, be more specific about how much money you'd like to put away and by when, for example: in three months' time I will have saved a specified amount of money.

For softer, less quantifiable goals such as having more fun or deepening your friendships, perhaps you could set a goal of certain activities to enjoy or all the ways you'd like to feel by a chosen target date.

Having specificity in this list will greatly increase your chances of meeting your goal and will help you to be able to track your progress in the action step opposite.

TAKE ACTION

Choose one thing from your list (perhaps the goal you'd most like to achieve) and track it every day for the next month.

You can track on a spreadsheet, enter your progress on a calendar, or write it on a piece of paper taped to your fridge.

Tracking is possible for any goal! If you're looking to save more money it's easily trackable because you'll analyze numbers from your bank account over a period of time. For this I'd recommend using a spreadsheet or a chart on the wall, whichever you're more likely to update regularly.

For improving softer areas of life such as 'having deeper friendships', you can assign number values or points to the activities or achievements related to the goal. For having deeper relationships, your numeric values could be:

A phone call with a friend: 50 points
Gave a thoughtful gift: 40 points
Sent a thank-you note: 30 points

Ideally you'll track your progress daily. During this process, you may notice certain things that keep cropping up and getting in the way of achieving your goal - maybe all you need is a few boundaries in place to help you achieve what you really want! Once you see your progress, you'll be motivated to continue and less likely to get tripped up by outside influences. Let's get tracking!

41

Save the best for now

This list aims to help you enjoy all the lovely, luxury things in your home that you rarely use because you're saving them for 'good'.

A friend told me a sad story of her father saving a bottle of champagne for thirty years, because he was waiting for the perfect special occasion to pop the cork. When he passed away, she opened the bottle to celebrate his life, only to find it had gone off and tasted like vinegar.

Allowing yourself to enjoy things that you deem luxury or special is an important part of self-care. If you don't think you're worth these things, what are you saying to your self-esteem? My point is, the special occasion is now. The special occasion is you!

Make a list of all the things you've been saving for 'good' or for a special occasion.

Your list can include items such as thoughtful gifts, expensive skincare, beautiful clothes, fancy tableware, scented luxury candles. Look out for things still in their packaging or with tags left on them, and be sure to account for the smaller items such as jewellery or cufflinks.

It's like going on a treasure hunt of your own stuff! Go through your home and find the items hidden away in drawers or at the back of a cupboard and add them to your list. While you're there, bring them forward to be put in regular use.

TAKE ACTION

Using these items will boost your mood and self-image, and make you feel like the deserving person you are. Treat yourself to a skincare session with a potion you had left sitting on a shelf. Light all the lovely candles you have and bask in the glow. Wear your luxury clothing and accessories on your next shopping trip.

If you're hoarding gifts that were given to you, ask yourself why you're not indulging in them. Notice your mindset – do you feel like you'll never get such a lovely treat again? I assure you, there are always more scented candles coming your way, and you deserve this now.

I have a gorgeous crystal bowl that was given to me as a gift years ago, and it's so fancy that I'd never used it because I was afraid I'd break it. It sat in a cupboard for ages and its beauty was hidden away. Recently, I took it out, washed it, placed it on my kitchen table and filled it with fresh lemons. It adds so much style and cheer to the room and it makes everything around it look more charming and higher quality.

What are you waiting for?

42

Radiate positive energy

It's a powerful practice to wake up with the intention of positivity, no matter what your mood. Whether you know it or not, you have the option to change your perspective at any time, even if you're feeling 'meh' or pretty bad.

This list helps you get in the habit of waking up hopeful and bright, helpful and strong. You will feel great throughout your day and notice that things seem to be easier for you when you're keeping this mindset. The best side-effect of this is that you will radiate positivity to others, and your bright attitude will catch on!

Make a list of 20 ways you can bring positivity into your day.

You could recite an inspiring mantra upon waking and share it with others, you could make a gratitude list, you could check in with someone you love and tell them you hope they have a great day. Simply bringing a smile to your face as soon as you wake up will set the tone for the day. Later on, take some mindfulness breaks to appreciate all the aspects of your life, such as the people you love, or how fortunate you are to be where you are.

Every morning, the first thing I do is drink a big glass of water. I imagine I'm a garden that needs this life force to grow and flourish throughout the day. I love this little routine because it really inspires me to feel like there are so many possibilities to look forward to, all my projects and moments ahead are like my flowers and fruit trees.

If you're struggling to come up with ideas for yourself, start from scratch – simply realizing that we are all lucky to be alive is a good place to build on. Anytime you come up with a negative thought, flip it on its head. For instance, if your mind says, 'ugh I don't want to go to work today', say to yourself, 'I'm going to really enjoy work today'.

TAKE ACTION

Commit to bringing one item on your list into every day for the next month.

A good trick here is to start as soon as you wake up, otherwise it's easy to just get into your normal groove and forget. Some days will be harder than others, and your mind and body will tell you that it's impossible to flip your negative script. If you can't shake your mood, then it's time to bring in the big dogs – pull up a silly dance class on YouTube and move your body, play some uplifting music, watch some comedy.

I recommend adopting my big glass of water habit, because staying hydrated helps you think more clearly and gives you a better chance of noticing your thought patterns.

Remember that happiness is a practice, and it's up to you to stay on top of it. You have the power to shape your outlook and maintain a positive approach to your day.

43

Step into your ideal life

Your entries from this list will come from a guided visualization, where I ask you to imagine your ideal life while engaging all your senses.

Close your eyes for a few minutes and imagine you have achieved everything you've wanted and that you are now living your ideal life. Perhaps this is in 3–5 years' time, you're still close in age to where you are now but you've managed to reach your goals in a quick and fabulous way. I want you to mentally walk through this life on your typical ideal day.

If you're at home, notice how it's decorated, the energy of the space, perhaps there's a window open letting in a cool breeze, perhaps you've got candles burning. Feel your clothes as you walk around your day, notice who you'll spend your time with, what you'll eat for lunch, the sound of birds in the garden. Check into your senses and take note of this ideal existence.

Make a list of everything you saw, smelled, felt, tasted, heard. Write down any details such as the light, where you were in the world, any sounds you noticed, your mood.

Envisaging your ideal life in a relaxed, meditative state allows the mind to run free and creatively design how you really want to live. Perhaps you see yourself in a luxury tracksuit sitting beside a fireplace in your gorgeous chalet in the mountains, which overlooks a sparkling lake. Or in a refurbished ranch house in Austin, footsteps away from all the nightlife and taco stands, your walls are lined with your record collection, and you own multiple pairs of sequinned cowgirl boots.

I absolutely love making this list because I'm such a fantasist. In my vision, I'm wearing a silk kaftan and my personal chef is making me the salad of my dreams. There's spa music in the background and outside my large French doors to the patio are a blue sky and peaceful ocean in view. My friends are coming over later for tequila-based cocktails and karaoke. I could go on and on, but my point here is to dream big.

 **T A K E   A C T I O N**

Choose items from your list to incorporate into your life every day for the next month.

Sometimes our ideal life is already at our fingertips. We tend to hold ourselves back because we don't feel we're ready for, or maybe don't deserve, our ideal lives. It's time to take those dreams and design them into our reality now.

You may have to budget, save, hustle for it, but that luxury tracksuit could actually be yours now if you wanted it. You could visit a chalet in the mountains by a lake, and start building upon your record collection now. There should be some sequinned cowgirl boots in your closet already! Ideal life, realized!

44

Try new things

We are all creatures of habit, we tend to stick to activities and behaviours that we've become used to over time. We're probably going for the tried-and-true for a variety of reasons, including social anxiety or lack of imagination. Getting out of our comfort zone and trying new things will shake us up and open our minds to the countless possibilities around us.

Trying a new thing can be daunting at first, but it doesn't have to be that way. Feel free to only include things that sound fun to you on this list; you can add in the scarier stuff next time.

Make a list of interesting things to do that you've never tried before.

This list can include a wide array of activities and projects, such as cooking a new recipe for a dish you've never tried, exploring a new genre of music, watching foreign movies, trying a new workout routine, going to a networking event. If you're brave, you could add more adventurous ideas such as skydiving, rock climbing or cold water swimming.

TAKE ACTION

Choose one of the items from your list and give it a try in the next month.

Okay, trying to fit in skydiving in the next month might be a little bit harrowing, but for a lot of your entries you'll have no problem achieving the brief.

You could set aside a Saturday afternoon to listen to a particular genre of music that you're unfamiliar with. Perhaps a friend can join you for a food-foraging workshop, or meet you to explore a different neighbourhood in your city.

Just like everyone else, I can be quite stuck in my ways as far as this list goes. I can tend to limit my exploration for a myriad of reasons and they're mostly nonsense. I can sometimes feel too busy or too lazy to try something different, or I think I've already discovered the best of everything, so why take a risk? Often I don't even know I'm blocking an opportunity for a new experience.

Usually it takes a friend to suggest a new activity, such as taking part in an online detective mystery game or going kayaking. This list aims to help us be that friend for ourselves.

45

Embrace beauty

Wherever you live, whether it be in the centre of a city, surrounded by suburbs or in open countryside, you are enveloped by beauty. Taking the time to observe things you find beautiful is an act of pleasure and a basic human need. This list reminds us to take pleasure in observing the world around us, and that beauty can be found more easily than you think.

Make a list of the most beautiful things in your town, city or neighbourhood.

This list can include local parks that were planned to perfection with gorgeous trees, clusters of plants and flowers and meandering pathways. You could add examples of local architecture and houses that you admire. Perhaps you live near a museum that is filled with art, sculpture and design. You can include whatever you feel is beautiful, and this can include people, streets, shops, restaurants and even atmospheres.

I live near a street where a few of the houses have really worked on their gardens, lawns and flowering plants. I make an effort to walk my dog Marlowe down this street so I can marvel at their perfect scented roses or the topiary trimmed to look like a goldfish, and to smell the honeysuckle in spring.

Also in my neighbourhood is an old barber's shop, and its sign looks like it was made in the 70s. I love the design of the typeface and the blue and red colours of the plastic lettering. Because it's on a corner, the shop has windows on two sides, allowing a clear

view of the wood-panelled walls and dated photographs of sample haircuts. It looks like it's been trapped in time and I think it's gorgeous.

TAKE ACTION

Choose one source of beauty from your list to visit, appreciate and savour this month.

Block out time in your schedule this month to really enjoy yourself as you revel in the form, shape, detail, colour and atmosphere of your subject. Consult with yourself as to why you find it beautiful, and notice the thoughts and feelings that arise.

You could write a journal as you observe, take a photo or record a voice note if you'd like to keep a record of your savouring. You may even feel compelled to be creative and sketch or paint the object, which is only a good thing! Let it flow.

Studies show that when we are exposed to the beauty of nature, culture and art, it builds resilience, enhances healing and promotes our creativity. Furthermore, the lighthearted feeling we get when we are taking in something that is gorgeous is a wonderful coping mechanism and boosts our mood.

If you apply this approach in your local area, you also benefit from a strong connection to your surroundings and community, which will in turn strengthen your sense of belonging.

46

Pleasure

The mention that having sex makes us happy might sound obvious, but I'm including this exercise because engaging and exploring our sensual side is a big factor in our wellness and maintaining our life fulfilment. It's a necessary part of human life, and research shows that having positive sexual relationships, with ourselves or others, is key to maintaining our life satisfaction. Studies have proven that on the days we've had sex or engaged in self-pleasure, we report increased levels of happiness.

Bringing a healthy sexuality practice to your life is excellent for your physical health, it activates your cardiovascular system, releases happy hormones like serotonin, oxytocin and endorphins, and it relieves stress. Exploring our sensuality can bring about increased self-worth, better confidence in our bodies and teach us more about nurturing ourselves and others.

We can learn so much about ourselves through exploring this way, and safe, consensual sex with someone we trust (or by ourselves) can be a playground of creativity and self-expression. Allow yourself the pleasure you deserve!

List three ways you'd like to increase your sexual and sensual pleasure.

Remember, the items on your list don't have to involve other people, you can feel free to devote your entries to self-love.

You can add new things you'd like to try, and be more adventurous with your exploration of all things sensual. You can add to your list something that you already know makes you feel wonderful, and just do it more often.

TAKE ACTION

This month, choose one of the entries from your list, and indulge.

Set aside ample time this month to explore and expand your pleasures for increased happiness. This is all about enjoying yourself and taking the time for discovery.

You can set the stage for your session by lighting candles, putting on music and doing all your favourite self-care practices to feel relaxed and ready to indulge. Whether you have a partner or not, there is always plenty of scope for trying new things and finding out what's exciting for you.

Expanding your pleasure horizons will not only improve your wellness, but you'll feel loved up, more confident in your body and you'll be glowing inside and out!

47

Help yourself win

There are always going to be hiccups to stop you from completing tasks on the path to your goals. Know yourself, know your excuses and stop them before they happen! Even more powerfully, we can use foresight and planning to set up our lives to make the process easier. This list helps us define how we can change our environment, habits and routines to better reach our goals.

A common pitfall is when people set themselves the goal of regular exercise, but just can't seem to get there. They wake up and find their gym kit is in the washing machine, or they lost track of time scrolling through social media and missed a spinning class. Whoops! With a little self-awareness and forward planning, this could have been avoided.

Make a list about how you can adjust your home or daily routine to give yourself shortcuts (or more likely, pathways) to reach your goals.

Add to your list some daily activities that would support the life you're shooting for. Mentally go through your typical day for the past week or so. You may notice there are some activities in your life that are actually hindering your progression, so we'll aim to swap them out for things that are helpful.

For instance, if your goal is that you want to work out more, you could make sure you have easy access to your workout clothes by setting them out at night for the next day. Also, you could make sure you have enough outfits so you don't have to do laundry in order to work out this often. Put your phone next to your gym kit – you can scroll later!

There will be some non-negotiable activities that should be on your list. For instance, if you want to meet new people you have to be around... new people. So you could perhaps work from a local coffee shop instead of working from home.

 **T A K E   A C T I O N**

Choose three items from your list and put them into action this month.

Set yourself up for success by turning some items from this list into reality. Get creative in finding ways to put the odds of reaching your goals back in your favour.

You could set yourself phone reminders to prepare your gym kit the night before. You could look out for some cool coffee shops with good seating and strong wifi, and walk in with a big smile on your face. Don't forget, you can always help yourself by asking and/or paying others for support, hiring in services or setting up subscriptions. For instance, renting a hot desk at a shared office space and attending their social events will find you meeting new people instantly. Having your personal trainer come to your home is a surefire way to keep you committed!

48

Favourite analogue games

We spend so much time on our phones and laptops, and while we do use these tools to connect to people, it's no replacement for the joy we feel by spending time with each other in real life. Studies show that when people look at their phones, others assume they do not want to connect and will not engage with them. So we're desperately trying to connect but alienating people at the same time? Ugh!

Social networking can be a minefield – sometimes it can help us feel more connected to people, but mostly all this screen time leaves us comparing ourselves to others (and their exceptionally edited versions of themselves). The same goes for online gaming, which is fun, but no replacement for the human interaction of good ol' fashioned board games.

It's time to take a tech break and play like the kids of yesteryear.

Make a list of your favourite games that are analogue (AKA old-school, not requiring a phone, game console or computer).

These can include board games, card games, puzzles, trivia, dice, dominoes. Your list can be made up of games you know and love, but also games you'd like to try or learn.

The regular practice of playing games can increase self-esteem and help battle stress, build intellect and treat grief. As long as it doesn't require solitude and a battery charger, it's safe to go on this list.

TAKE ACTION

Bring out your inner child and play some games this month.

Invite friends, family, your partner to play these games with you. It can be a games night in your home, in a park, on Zoom, or make a plan to bring a game and visit them. Be sure to make a 'no phones' rule, and have everyone put theirs away.

These days, I find many pubs and bars have board games, and here in London some are even board game-themed! There are also board game events happening at the lovelier quirky venues, allowing guests to mix the joy of playing games with meeting new people and making social connections. In the game of happiness, everyone wins!

It's crazy how much fun you can have with just a set of dice – we play regular games of Farkle with our dear friends Nick and Amanda. I love battling my husband over a game of Tangoes, a game where you place shaped tiles to match an image from a card deck. I can still lose hours playing Rummy, a game I learned from my childhood best friend Celeste.

49

Laser-focused single-tasking to achieve your dreams

This list is the autobahn of dream realization. If you want to get something done, you've got to clear the distractions and roadblocks and focus on it. It's like being in university when you've left yourself just two hours to turn in your term paper – we've all done it.

I'll share a little hack to bring in the countdown timer, the manager making you stick to a deadline, the client saying they needed it yesterday. But first, let's set the stage:

Make a list of your biggest, loftiest goals and dreams for your life – career-based, personal or around your relationships.

You can include the stuff that feels really far away, like you're at point A and the goal is point W. The aim here is that we are going to find out what happens when we actually pursue with laser focus.

TAKE ACTION

Choose one of these goals and laser-focus on it.

Map out all the steps you'd need to take to reach this goal.

For the next month, complete as many of these steps as possible. Do not fall prey to imposter syndrome. Keep to the deadline of one month and see how far you go.

If, for instance, you wanted to become a film director, you could plan backwards from there and watch tutorials and take courses on the subject, make your own short film, and submit it to local film festivals. The point here is to 'try it on' and act like you are definitely going to reach this goal.

If you change your mind halfway through and decide you don't want to become a film director, keep going anyway. This will solidify the belief in yourself that you can focus on a goal for an entire month and follow your own prescribed course of action. You will learn a lot on the way, especially about yourself. You can always try to achieve a new dream next month!

When I first wanted to start my own business, I delved deep in research and took some courses to learn exactly what would be involved in the process. I actually started two businesses before I landed on the one that is a current success, but all the learning from my first forays definitely helped me get to this point. The trick is to focus and keep going!

50

Bucket list activated

The bucket list is probably the second most popular list, after the to-do list, and there's even been a Hollywood movie made about it! In case you didn't know, a bucket list consists of all the things you'd like to do before you kick the bucket. Yes, it's a bit morbid, but I think most people work best with a deadline (pun intended).

It can be a tough exercise to come up with all the things you'd like to do while you're alive, especially when you have your whole life ahead of you. Therefore, for this version of the bucket list I've given you one year, because we can all tend to put things off, especially when it comes to our life enjoyment and dreams.

Make a list of all the things you'd do if you had one year to achieve them.

Having only one year as a timeline really lights a fire underneath you and gets your creativity working on how to pull off these dreams.

Your list can be made up of adventures, focus time with family, far-flung travel, learning a new skill or facing a fear. You can include things you never got around to, like learning how to ice skate, or places you've never seen, like the pyramids of Giza. My list is always full of travel, experiences and entertainment. I'd love to visit various animal sanctuaries around the world, go to Mardi Gras in New Orleans, watch figure skating at the Olympics and be in the audience at Eurovision. I've always wanted to 'collect' all the new seven wonders, especially Machu Picchu.

TAKE ACTION

Choose one item from your list and in the next month, commit and plan it into your life within the next year.

There's no time like the present, so you could book yourself ice-skating lessons at your local rink and be pretty good at skating in a couple of months. You could research your trip to Egypt to see the pyramids and budget for your booking with a tour operator.

It's helpful to keep this list on hand, because as your life unfolds you'll see ways to achieve your list items as opportunities present themselves.

For instance, it was always on my bucket list to visit Dollywood, which is located in Tennessee. I live in London, which is not exactly nearby, so this remained on my list for years. Then, when my friends Kelsey and Ray announced their wedding would take place in Nashville, I saw my opportunity and also booked a couple of extra days to drive across the state to Dollywood. If it wasn't on my list for so long, I might have talked myself out of taking the extra time. I'm so glad I did!

51

Holiday, celebrate!

Do you ever get the feeling that a certain holiday or birthday has come around so quickly, and you feel underprepared for it? Much of the happiness we get from celebrations comes from the exciting build-up and preparation stage.

This list will help us plan celebrations ahead so we can really savour the approach and better enjoy the actual occasion itself.

Celebrations help us build and maintain a strong connection to our family, friends and community, and give us a sense of belonging. When planning for these moments, we engage our creativity and thoughtfulness and just thinking about a joyful celebration makes us smile.

Preparing for these holidays and moments provides me with such joy, and it's why I chose to work in event design. I love thinking about every aspect of an occasion. Planning parties is such a wonderful way to practise kindness to your loved ones.

Make a list of all of the annual holidays, anniversaries, birthdays and occasions you plan to celebrate this year.

Your list can include religious holidays such as Christmas and Diwali, relationship anniversaries, birthdays, cultural holidays like Halloween, and awareness celebrations such as Indigenous Peoples' Day and International Women's Day. Just look online to find out what's happening when.

If you are having trouble finding occasions to celebrate, take a cue from social media and celebrate National Donut Day, International Yoga Day and World Bicycle Day!

TAKE ACTION

Add these dates to your calendar for the year, and plan some special, fun ways to celebrate the ones taking place in the next couple of months.

Envisage how you'd like to celebrate, and with whom. If it's a family birthday, you could message your family and start planning for it. If you're planning for a harvest festival, you could invite friends to join you on a hay ride or go pumpkin-picking.

Making advance plans to celebrate helps you carve out time to spend with your loved ones. It encourages you to have fun for fun's sake, and gives you things to look forward to. An antidote to the day-to-day routine, these celebrations provide a pause and opportunity to savour the life you've worked so hard to create. Before you know it, your calendar and life will be filled with fun, exciting get-togethers and you'll be connecting with the people you love more than ever before.

My husband and I celebrate everything possible, we love creating menus, decorating, making playlists, planning outfits. Looking forward to these celebrations definitely makes me happier, I leap from one to the other and let my creativity and thoughtfulness flow as I plan.

52

Get it done

Procrastination can be a bit poisonous. If you leave a project on your to-do list for too long, it can sometimes make you feel like a failure or that you can't trust yourself to complete tasks. It's not a big deal if you put off sewing a loose button onto a shirt, but if it makes you feel like you never complete anything, then that's a problem. This can leak into other areas of your life and leave you feeling awful.

Research has shown that procrastination not only affects our productivity, but also our mental and physical health. Issues like chronic stress, low life satisfaction, symptoms of depression and anxiety, poor health behaviours, chronic illness and even hypertension are linked to procrastination. It's definitely in your best interest to get it done!

This list will help you get these tasks off your mind once and for all, so you can get back to living your happy, productive life.

Make a list of all the tasks, chores and projects that have been kicking around for way too long.

We all have things on our to-do list that we dread, or they're just the right amount of annoying that we leave them on there. It can be tasks like updating your LinkedIn account, fixing something in your house that's broken or clearing out the junk drawer.

You can include small things like personal chores, professional tasks, life admin, as well as larger milestone things like moving house, changing your car or finding a new job.

I've been fighting against my own procrastination for years and I've become pretty good at keeping it at bay. When you run your own business, putting things off causes pain to you and only you, so I've mastered either tackling a task or handing it over to someone else.

Personally though, I have lots of little things that have been piling up. In my jewellery box I have a selection of necklaces, bracelets and earrings that have lost a link or need to be fixed in some way. I also own jewellery-making tools, so I could just sit down and fix these things, but I just haven't got around to it.

I'd say there is a junk drawer in every room of my home, and every time I open one I get mildly frustrated – this is totally going on my list.

 **TAKE ACTION**

Do yourself a favour and blast these tasks this month!

It's time to get it done! Take a good hard look at this list and decide which of these items you can tackle immediately, and delete or delegate the things that you know will never get done.

If you listed any household tasks, you could set aside half an hour each weekend this month to focus on and complete them. Put some music on and clean that refrigerator. You can also delegate tasks to your housemate or partner, by posting up a list of home projects that need completing and asking them to sign up for half of them.

If you're focusing on a work-related or professional task, overcome whatever is holding you back and blast it! Perhaps you need some more information or advice to mark this as complete, or to get a team together to tackle it.

For the larger tasks like finding a new home or job, don't forget that you can ask for help. You can call up an estate agent and provide them with your 'must have' list, and get in touch with a recruitment firm in your chosen industry and tell them about your dream job.

I've just set myself a calendar reminder to go through my broken jewellery this weekend and get it fixed once and for all. I'm going to 'treat myself' to some wooden organizers for my junk drawers, so at least my junk is beautifully displayed.

Once you free up your mind, you'll feel wonderful and able to move forward. Your confidence in yourself will be off the chart, and you'll notice the low-level stress you were suffering is alleviated.

53

The best years of your life

This list uses the power of creative visualization and intention-setting and applies it to your happiness levels for the future. If you can envisage how you'd like to spend your time, with whom and in what setting as you grow old, you'll more clearly see your values and priorities.

Also, if you can imagine specifics on how you'd like to live out your life, you're more likely to be able to bridge the gap between the way you're living now and where you want to be.

List out all the different aspects of the best years of your life (they haven't happened yet!).

How would your life play out in a best-case scenario?

Perhaps you see yourself travelling the world with your partner, or living in an adorable village, running a coffee shop, making friends with the locals and living a simple peaceful life. Maybe you see yourself as living exactly where you are, with the same people, but there's a more fun, harmonious environment.

You don't have to imagine yourself as much older than you are, because the goal is to live the best years of your life and build on them. Studies show we get happier as we get older, so this is a great way to get a head start.

One of the big lessons we learn from this exercise is that when we paint the picture of the best years of our lives, we may notice that in our current lives, there are some glaring omissions. Or that some things just need a little nudge.

For instance, on my list is the entry: 'lots of time spent relaxing and exercising with the people I love in the sun'. This is pretty far off how I'm living my life on a regular basis, the sun is a fleeting visitor here in London and a lot of the people I love are back in New York.

Also on my list is 'I volunteer often and give lots of money to charities'. I always imagine myself as a rich and generous old lady who gets really involved with her chosen causes. While I make small charity donations regularly, and try to increase this yearly, I could spend more of my time volunteering.

 **TAKE ACTION**

If you imagined yourself travelling the world with your partner, you could plan a smaller more achievable trip this month. If you envisaged running the coffee shop and making friends with the locals in your village, you could go to your local coffee shop and chat to the person sat next to you. If you pictured a more fun, harmonious life with your friends and family, you could schedule in a games night or a relaxed pizza party.

For my examples, I could probably turn this into reality now by making more regular visits to see my family and loved ones back in New York, and making more plans with them to go hiking and swimming in the sun. I could budget for this every year, and maybe save money on renting a holiday house if I planned in advance. I could research and apply for a volunteering role for a cause I'm passionate about.

You may need a longer plan in place to make the things on your list happen, but by taking the first steps now, you are giving yourself a better chance of living your best years as you've envisaged them. Let's all plan a pizza party this month, regardless!

54

Smell the roses

There's lots of research linking sense of smell with memory and emotion, and perfumes and fragrances have been used for mood boosting for centuries. Data from one study found that its participants used three times as many happiness-related words when asked to recall life events in a floral-scented room. Putting science aside, we know that something that smells good to us instantly makes us happy. Nature provides us with so many delightful scents, such as the smell of the earth after rain, the waft of honeysuckle in spring, the salty air of a sunny day at the beach.

With this list, we'll be engaging the sense of smell to increase your happiness and life enjoyment.

Make a list of your favourite happiness-inducing fragrances.

Add to this list all the scents that cheer you up or make you feel a sense of lovely nostalgia. Your entries can include anything from freshly mown grass or the smell of chocolate chip cookies baking in the oven, to your favourite perfume. There may be good reason behind some of your entries, for instance the smell of citrus fruits has been proven to boost moods and sharpen the mind, and vanilla is known to give us a comforting feeling.

My favourite smells include freshly ground coffee, the multi-layered fragrance of health-food stores and the romantic scent of a peony flower. And I love the smell of pumpkin pie spices, as they make me think of all the years spent celebrating holidays with my grandmother, Bertha, who was a baker extraordinaire.

TAKE ACTION

Commit to bringing a few of the scents from your list into your life this month.

It might take a bit of legwork to find the freshly mown grass, but you could bake yourself some chocolate chip cookies and enjoy this multi-sensory cuddle.

You can find aromatherapy oils for many of your favourite scents to put in a burner or diffuser, to dab at your pulse points or pour into your bath. If you save your favourite perfume and only wear it for special occasions, this month simply wear it for yourself.

Take some time to engage your senses, emotions and memories through exploring your favourite fragrances. Savouring and enjoying the sensory aspects of our lives will boost your mood and gratitude, and add layers of enjoyment to your days.

You can even build some of these olfactory indulgences into your every day. I found a candle scented with lemongrass, ginger and rosemary that really reminds me of that health-food store smell. My coffeemaker has a built-in grinder that is set to go off at the same time every morning, and the smell of freshly ground coffee lures me out of bed. To get my fix of pumpkin pie spices, I find quick access to that heartwarming smell by having a cup of chai tea almost every evening – it's like a hug from Bertha.

55

Give your time

Volunteering is magic. Not only are we helping the causes we care about, but when we volunteer we experience better mental and physical health, as well as increased social connection.

A study from the University of Exeter Medical School has proven that volunteering and helping others can improve our wellbeing, combat depression and even increase our life expectancy. In another study, participants reported a 'warm glow' and felt more connected to the world.

Whenever a friend or acquaintance seems to be constantly complaining, I always think, 'Wow, they need to do some volunteering'. I don't always say it aloud, but my problem-solving brain knows that this act would definitely get them off their pity pot. The thing is, unknowingly, we can all be that person throwing themselves a pity party from time to time, so having this list on hand is a great way to stop that from happening.

Make a list of causes and organizations for which you'd like to volunteer.

If you struggle to come up with ideas, think about the aspects of your local area or community that really get your goat, or desperately need improvement. Think about your values – if you're a passionate vegan you could volunteer for an animal sanctuary, if you are passionate about race and gender equality you could volunteer for an organization that lobbies and fights for this.

I'm a devoted volunteer for Democrats Abroad, who assist overseas Americans in voting and voter awareness. I plan fundraising events to help them get out the vote to as many people as possible. Our organization was one of the major influencing factors of the recent progressive election results, and I couldn't be prouder. Talk about a 'warm glow'!

TAKE ACTION

Choose one of these causes and look for volunteer opportunities on their website. Apply to volunteer this month.

If there aren't any listed, or you're not able to fulfil any of their volunteer roles, move down your list until you find something. For a home-grown approach, you can look for local organizations and charities that help the causes you're passionate about.

There are so many ways you can help different charities and organizations – some simply need admin support which you can do from home, or simple tasks like being a steward at an event. If you're a writer you can offer to help create social media posts, if you're naturally chatty you could volunteer to do some donor calls.

The uplift I get from planning fundraising events is wonderful. I'm using my natural skills, so it's not super challenging for me to give my time this way. Plus, I love working as a team with fellow Americans in London who share my values.

Find this level of fulfilment for yourself and get that warm glow!

56

Lead by example

You most likely already have some great behaviours around maintaining your own life-satisfaction, otherwise you wouldn't be so interested in the content of this book. Bravo, you!

This list is all about sharing the skills and knowledge you've learned about your own happiness with others, whether that be your friends, your co-workers, your family, your industry or your followers on social media.

When we see good examples of mindfulness, self-care, positivity and other healthy habits in our daily lives, the effect is contagious. We feel like this is the norm, and it helps us look after ourselves properly.

Make a list of your best behaviours, habits, actions and features that you'd love to inspire in others.

Perhaps you are the pinnacle of health with your daily yoga practice, or you're the person that always buys thoughtful presents for their friends.

On my list I added light-heartedness, kindness and good etiquette, which are definitely factors in my happiness, and I'd love to see more of this in others.

TAKE ACTION

Exhibit the items from your list and share your great example in full force this month.

Be a shining beacon of joy and fulfilment to those around you. Show off your best facets of self-care and happiness practices. Be a leader around living a life of fun, enjoyment, good health and strong personal connections.

For instance, if you listed your admirable daily yoga habit you could invite others to join you in a one-week challenge. If you're the expert gift-giver, you could team up with your friends and pool your money to buy someone a really thoughtful mega-gift.

My light-heartedness can change the energy of a room in a millisecond; I'll crack a joke, put on music or simply start smiling at people. I think sometimes people forget that feeling good is an option! I'm so glad to lead in the name of fun.

The practice of putting yourself in a leadership mindset also helps you overcome your own hang-ups and obstacles. When we put ourselves in the spotlight, we're more likely to exhibit the good behaviour we know we should be exhibiting.

57

Dance yourself happy

This is a fun list to make so that you're ready to surprise and delight your friends and loved ones at the next party, wedding or TikTok moment! Having a few dance tricks up your sleeve is a wonderful treat for yourself and others. Learning the moves to well-known line dances or iconic music videos is a great way to unlock a new level of fun in your life. Running a dance routine to music with friends is one of my most reliable forms of pleasure.

Studies have shown that dance positively impacts our physical and mental health, as well as improve interpersonal connection. Adding regular dance breaks to your life is not only healthy exercise, but you'll also feel happier and more loved!

Let's bust a move!

List five dance routines you want to learn.

You could choose dances from your favourite music videos, movies, musical theatre, even cartoons. If you're stumped, head on over to YouTube or TikTok for inspiration. There you will find dance routines aplenty, suitable for all fitness levels and for varying degrees of coordination.

You get extra credit if you come up with your own choreography – there's nothing better than seeing someone perform their made-up dance in a party situation.

Professionally, I perform the macarena, some 90s Britney video choreo and Whigfield's Saturday Night dance on a regular basis at my *Indeedy Bingo* shows. I often incite these dances at social events too – mass dancing in unison is truly soul-fulfilling and kicks the party up a notch.

 **T A K E   A C T I O N**

Choose one of these dances, and commit to learn and perfect it in the next month.

Depending on the length and detail of the dance, you'll need to commit sufficient time to learn the moves in front of the mirror, and then memorize and just 'feel' them. Let a few days pass and try doing the dance without a mirror, and see if you can still get it. You might need a bit more practice. Have fun!

Knowing these moves will impress friends and strangers, and you'll never be labelled a wallflower again. The world needs more dancers just like you.

To supercharge the positive effects of this exercise, rope in a friend or partner, or the whole family! You might find it so much fun you can tick off your entire list of dance routines in no time.

58

Write thank-you notes

Expressing gratitude is a proven method to increase happiness, and this can be achieved by writing a gratitude journal, or through a focused meditation, or by jotting down things you're grateful for as part of your bedtime routine. I try to practise all these things and recommend that you do too, because they really make a difference on your outlook.

But let's bring it back to basics. I believe there is a lot to say for the good ol' thank-you note, a formality that seems to be ever-diminishing in a world online where people are saying quick thanks through emails, social posts and texts.

Personally, I think any form of thank-you note is welcome, but the ones that come through the mail have a specialness to them. The people in my life that go through the trouble of hand-writing and sending me a thank-you note have won my heart forever.

Make a list of people you'd like to thank.

This list can include friends, family members, teachers, companies whose products have helped you.

If you're struggling to come up with a list, think of everyone who helped you get to where you are today. If a friend recently gave you good advice or listened to you when you needed to talk, they should go on this list. If someone's been a consistent inspiration, let them know. If anyone's given you a gift in the last year, better late than never!

 **TAKE ACTION**

Write thank-you notes to three of the recipients on your list this month.

It can be to say thanks for a gift, or thanking them for their friendship and support. You can write a note to an old co-worker who inspired you to seek the career you're in now. It can be to your favourite chocolate company to tell them how much you appreciate their work.

Be detailed in your thanks, describe how you feel, what you liked about it and how they've helped you. Sending a thank-you note will make your own heart light up, as well as the recipient's.

I love stationery, and always try to keep lovely thank-you notes and matching envelopes on hand. If I've run out, I take out a page from my watercolour book and cut it into postcard size for easy sending, and I write my note of gratitude on the back. Be sure to keep a book of stamps lying around.

59

Spend for happiness

No matter your income, studies have found that giving money or buying things for other people brings you happiness. You'd think 'well, it brings the other person happiness' and while that is likely true, it has been proven that spending money on others will definitely boost your mood.

Studies in all walks of life, from countries with very poor economies to wealthier countries with a higher average income, all found the same result. We feel great when we donate, and we feel better when we spend more on other people than when we buy stuff for ourselves.

Make a list of ways you can spend money on others.

This can include buying someone a drink, giving some money to a busker, supporting your friends' businesses (even though you may not need their products), or giving the local ice-cream man a large note when he stops on your street, and pay for all the neighbourhood kids' treats.

If your initial reaction is, 'Wait, I need all the money I make', is that really true? I'm sure you can forego some small change to start the ideas flowing, and build from there.

It's even better if the way you're donating or supporting charities also benefits you with social connection, or when you directly see the positive results of your generosity. Helping real people will boost happiness levels, such as sponsoring refugees or supporting local homeless organizations.

 **TAKE ACTION**

Put one of these items into action over the next month.

Again, this doesn't have to cost you a lot. The simple act of giving money to someone else, or buying them something will make you feel such fulfilment. It will be totally worth it.

I like to buy lunch for homeless people when I see them outside a supermarket. I love treating my friends to drinks and dinner every now and then. If I'm mindlessly shopping online on the sofa, sometimes instead of buying something I don't need, I send money to a charity I want to support. I'm sure that makes me feel a lot better than another cute top.

So the next time someone offers to buy you something, let them! You'll be doing their happiness a favour.

60

Get lost

There are constant scripts running in our heads; thoughts and emotions are repeatedly vying for our attention like barking puppies. When we take steps to help our busy minds chill out, we're more productive and happier in our daily lives.

There are certain 'mindless' activities that we can bring into our days that can calm inner chatter. In general, these activities are categorized as: sex, exercise, talking and conversation, listening to or playing music, walking, eating, meditation, cooking and play.

Give your brilliant, thoughtful mind a break with this exercise, and prepare to get lost.

Make a list of activities (based on the categories above) that always make you lose track of time and be completely in the moment.

You know your own personal style for each category, for instance if you're more likely to listen to music than sit and play a piano. Within each category there are many options, for 'exercise' you could drill it down to going cycling, taking a HIIT class or a fun online workout.

You could add an entry for cooking your favourite gnocchi recipe, listening to a new album or playing your favourite game. On my list is a good long conversation with my best friend Jimmy, going for a walk around my local park and eating a perfectly ripe mango from my local food shop.

 **TAKE ACTION**

Schedule in one hour a week this month to do some of these activities, and just lose yourself.

Give your head and mood the gift of a settled mind by incorporating the activities from your list into your life on a weekly basis this month. Schedule in time for yourself to engage in the peaceful nothingness.

I would like to take a moment to mention that I think meditation is mandatory for everyone. The proven mental and physiological health benefits are just exponential, but for me, I know I'm a calmer, happier person when I stick to my regular meditation practice. So please go back and add this to your list above!

You can even combine them, such as cooking while listening to music, walking and conversing with a friend, having sex while playing guitar (just joking!). Whatever list entry you choose, you'll be giving your hardworking, easily distracted mind a well-needed break.

61

Join the club

Joining a club that is based around your personal interests has multiple benefits, the most important of which is increased social connection. When we have strong social networks, our stress levels are reduced and our overall happiness increases. Studies have proven that people who have strong friendships and social connections have fewer health problems and live longer.

Of course, there's the main benefit that you'll be focusing and exploring a subject you are passionate about, but joining a group is also a great way to make more friends and meet like-minded people. You'll enjoy a true sense of community and belonging.

If this exercise is making you feeling a bit shy, don't forget that it's a good habit to push yourself out of your comfort zone. Remember that these clubs exist for the sole reason of bringing people together. They're there to be enjoyed. Surrounding yourself with positive people who are also enthusiastic about the things you love is a great way to maintain your life enjoyment.

Make a list of clubs, groups and organizations that are related to your interests.

There's something for everyone out there, from sports teams to cooking groups to social meet-ups for people who knit. You could list clubs that would make you feel more involved in your community, such LGBTQ+ groups, or your preferred form of activism, such as climate change meet-ups. Look within and think of your true interests when making this list.

I have first-hand knowledge of the benefits of joining a club. In 2014, I joined a wine club for American expat ladies in London. At first we were very organized and set a grape or a country for the theme and did structured tastings. We've all grown to be such close friends over the years that we rarely even talk about the wine anymore – we just can't wait to catch up with each other.

 **TAKE ACTION**

Choose one of these clubs or organizations on your list and join it this month.

Commit to joining one of these and approach going to the first event with an open heart and a smile. You're going to have so much fun!

If you're struggling to decide which one to join, first try the one that seems easiest for you. There is no limit on the number of clubs you can belong to by the way, so get yourself out there! You may have to pay a small fee or membership dues, but this will be well worth it for the camaraderie.

People always assume that others don't want to be approached and chatted to, but this isn't true. There's something about being in a club that just makes conversation flow easier. You're still talking to strangers at first, but it feels safer because you're all there for the same purpose.

62

Travel, but locally

It's funny that when we travel, we're so relaxed and open about visiting new restaurants and trying new things. We have conversations with the barista in the coffee shop, befriend the bartender, learn the life story of a local. We are more ready to try new things and meet more people than we are in our own towns.

When we get back home, this open behaviour subsides and we're less curious about the same sorts of businesses and people that exist around us. This list aims to help you appreciate your local area, but with the eyes of an excitable, open-minded tourist.

Make a list of local businesses you'd like to visit and support.

You can add coffee shops, antique stores, corner stores, restaurants, cocktail bars, record shops and whatever else you fancy. Your list can also include service-based businesses such as printers, dry cleaners, hair salons and florists. If you're having trouble thinking of examples, you could go for an afternoon walk in your neighbourhood and look for some ideas. Or just get out Google Maps and do some street viewing.

I try to support as many small businesses as I can to preserve the unique character of my neighbourhood. I'm lucky to be surrounded by some really great businesses – there's an award-winning pâtisserie up the street, as well as one of the best fish and chip shops in London. My local produce store has perfectly merchandised fruits and vegetables, and I visit it almost every day.

TAKE ACTION

Schedule in when you're going to visit these spots, and when you're there, make an effort to chat to the owners and staff. Introduce yourself, say you live locally and pay them a compliment on their shop or business. You can ask them how they started, or what's next for their business, or if this is their busy season. Act like a wide-eyed tourist!

Visiting businesses and restaurants in your area with the curiosity of a vacationer is a great way to feel a sense of community, help your local economy and make some new friends. Before you know it, you'll feel like a true part of your neighbourhood, and you'll find yourself high-fiving people on the street!

Living in a city where most people ignore their neighbours can make it hard to connect locally unless you make a concerted effort, but I'm so glad I do this. There have been a couple of occasions where my befriending of local businesses has been invaluable, such as holding a spare key for a houseguest, or letting me use their phone when mine got stolen.

63

Shared experiences

It's been proven that we gain more happiness from spending money on experiences rather than physical things. Our enjoyment for material possessions decreases significantly over time, but the appreciation for our past experience increases.

Research has also shown that we encounter a higher level of enjoyment when we share experiences with others. For instance, a wine will taste better when you're at a wine tasting with friends (or even strangers), than when you imbibe alone. Seeing live music is definitely more epic when there's a crowd, and the heightened enjoyment still happens even amongst strangers. A recent study from the University of Rochester found that 'fun is more fun when others are involved'. So if you want to really enjoy something to the maximum, you had best involve other people.

This list will help you find ways to get the most out of your life and experiences by coming up with things that you can enjoy with others.

Make a list of experiences you'd like to share with others.

You can turn almost anything into a shared experience, but for this list I'd like you to come up with ideas that are totally your style.

For instance, if you're a sports fanatic you could add 'go see a baseball game with my sister', if you're an art-lover, you could list 'invite my friends to an art exhibition'. These experiences can be in your local area, involve travel or take place online.

On my list, I've included that I'd love to treat my team to a drag brunch, go on a hike with my family and visit France's first Michelin-starred vegan restaurant with my husband. If they allow my dog Marlowe into the restaurant, I'll probably gain enough happiness to last me a decade!

 **TAKE ACTION**

Commit to making one of the shared experiences from your list happen this month.

It's time to bring these into your reality! Involve friends, family or a group of people to join you in one of these adventures.

Some might take more advance planning than others and that's okay, but it would be great if you could actually enjoy one of these experiences this month. Heck, enjoy them all if you can! This is a 'the more the merrier' situation, literally.

For my examples, the quickest and easiest to plan is the drag brunch, so I'll do some research on possible dates this month at my favourite place, and then send a message to my team to see if they're free then. For the vegan restaurant, I'll start research for a trip later this year by looking at travel routes, local places to stay and other fun things to add into the trip. And maybe a petit phone call to the restaurant to ask '*autorisez-vous les chiens*?'.

It's good to have these experiences listed out and planned in the hopper, so you've got fun with friends in your future.

64

Spread the love

Making this list gives me such a warm and fuzzy feeling. Coming up with ways that we can express our love creatively is a heart-warming exercise, and really puts us in a generous, caring mindset.

It's so important to nurture the relationships you've got, and also to nurture the love of yourself. With this practice, you're keeping up good hygiene for your capacity to love. As you define ways to creatively show your love for others, your heart will fill up in the process.

The act of giving releases oxytocin in the brain, the hormone that makes you feel love and connection with others. Science says spread the love!

Make a list of ten people you love, and next to each name add ways you can show them your love and appreciation.

This list can include your partner, latest heartthrob, dear friends, family members, fur baby and whoever else you love. Your ideas can be for birthdays and special occasions, but try to design them for any old day and 'just because'. Feel free to add yourself to this list, and get ready to spoil yourself to oblivion.

I love making this list because it takes me out of my own head when I start thinking of how I can delight others. I go into creative mode while I think up lots of ways to be thoughtful for the people I love, and that's my happy place.

TAKE ACTION

Choose at least one entry from your list and make it happen this month.

Perhaps you added a friend on the list who's been super supportive recently and you'd like to say thank you. Or a parent who has always been your best cheerleader and you'd like to show them your appreciation.

I know that my friend Katey absolutely loves to be given thoughtful little presents now and again, I've seen her delight when others have given her a bar of chocolate or her favourite drink. This month, I will surprise her with some little treats wrapped in some hand-printed wrapping paper to show her how much I love her.

My husband Charles is like a cuddly otter, he just wants to be smooshed up all the time, and he loves when I bake him things. So this month I will make sure I build in lots of time for otter cuddles and I'll make him his favourite Victoria sponge cake.

65

Take a break

Most of us struggle to switch off. We live in a culture where productivity is key, and we're flooded with advice on how to get the most out of our work days. Even at home, we're easily distracted by chores, side hustles and caring for others that we forget to give ourselves a break.

Recharging is a valuable part of life enjoyment, because it lowers your stress levels and resets your mood. Attention over-achievers: taking regular breaks has actually been proven to increase your productivity!

If you've mastered the art of stopping, I salute you. If not, now's your chance to identify and define ways to help yourself take a moment to recharge.

Make a list of ways you can stop and relax throughout your day.

Your list can include having a cup of tea, cuddling your pet or simply getting away from your desk to go outside to stand in the sun. You can add more involved ways to chill out such as guided meditation, taking a bubble bath or going for a long walk.

If you work from home, you could find a comfortable place to be with your thoughts. If you're at a workplace, find a quiet place to sit, put on some relaxing music in your headphones and breathe. Try not to involve screens, because you likely spend more than enough time with them.

One of my favourite ways to take a break is to put on some music and stretch on the floor. Working from home it's easy for me to do this, and it's become a habit over the years. My shoulders tell me when it's time to step away from the laptop.

The to-do list can wait, it's time to prioritize rest and recharge with the take-a-break list instead.

 **TAKE ACTION**

This month, set yourself a goal of taking one of these breaks every day.

Try all the different ways you've listed so you can find your favourites, and form a habit of regularly switching off. You can set specific times for your breaks, or just take one when you feel a natural pause in your day. If your mind races as you sit down with your cup of tea, just jot your thoughts down on a piece of paper, or shoo them away from your mind and continue to relax.

As you go, you'll discover more ways to relax everyday, so be sure to add them to your list.

Having a dog really helps me take a break – Marlowe takes me for regular walks outside and is so cute I can't help but take a minute to stop and play with him. More powerful than any phone reminder I've ever set!

66

Lighten up

This might sound obvious, and maybe a bit cyclic, but people who have more laughter and fun in their lives are happier.

Simply smiling causes your brain to secrete endorphins (the happy hormone), and laughter physiologically benefits you the same way exercise does. Laughter also allows the release of emotions, which crying does as well, but which would you rather do?!

I've seen the benefits of lightness and laughter in practice, because I'm a professional at lightening people's moods. I've spent over a decade creating events that allow people to relax, let their hair down and have fun with their friends and colleagues. As the host of these events, I show through my own behaviour that it's okay to let go and not take yourself too seriously. Everyone follows suit because freedom to feel joy is contagious.

Even a simple joke or meme can quickly change our mood, and subsequently, the course of our day. Let's make sure you've got lots of these methods at the ready.

Make a list of ways you can bring humour, lightness and laughter into your life on a regular basis.

Your list can include going to see or watching videos from your favourite comedians, going dancing to cheesy pop music, listening to a silly podcast, reminiscing on a funny memory with a friend or going to a karaoke night and marvelling at the sheer joy and variation of vocal techniques.

Think of things that bring you to a light, cheerful, giggly state. A quick cure could be to seek out some blooper reels from your favourite TV shows.

You know what makes you lighten up or laugh hardest, so add your tried-and-true methods to this list. You can build this list over time as you discover new gems. You could ask your friends for their funniest videos/memes/shows/podcasts etc. to grow your collection.

This is also a good opportunity to mention that if a certain friend in your life makes you laugh consistently, you should do whatever you can to keep that friendship for life!

There's also a new form of yoga called 'Laughter Yoga', where participants fake their laughing as part of the practice, and reap all the same physical and mental-health benefits as if they were truly laughing at something funny.

I am a disciple of Pee Wee Herman, a comedy actor who first became famous in the 80s with his TV show *Pee Wee's Playhouse*, and then his feature movie, *Pee Wee's Big Adventure*. His colourful, light-hearted, bonkers take on life was so inspiring to me that I've tried to carry his spirit within me ever since. His shows and movies are so inclusive, irreverent and off-the-wall. If ever I need a mood boost, his work is definitely one of my main sources.

I also have a Post-it Note on my mirror in the bedroom that says 'smile, be light' as a reminder to let go of any heaviness I'm carrying around.

TAKE ACTION

Bring at least three of your entries into your life this month.

This one should be so easy! Choose three ideas on your list and weave them into your life on a regular basis. If you can create a habit of bringing lightness to your life, you've won the game.

I'll bet many of your ideas could be accessed from your tech, and what a better way to spend your screen time than comparing yourself to all the unrealistic Instagram fakery. Download the entire series of a podcast you love to your phone so you have quick access to it. Save your go-to funny TV shows to your favourites so you're reminded to click play. Add a channel on YouTube to one of your bookmarks and go down that hilarious rabbit hole.

Set reminders to call that hilarious friend and have a good laugh. Write yourself a reminder and put it in plain view so that every day you are regularly uplifted!

67

Ask for help, free up time

Sometimes we can get caught up in doing everything ourselves, because we're multi-talented and one can learn how to do everything online. But in reality, we all have blind spots in our lives where our approach is substandard or just isn't working, and we would benefit from bringing in some extra help.

When we ask for help, we free up more of our time to spend on areas of life that matter. We're more effective at work, have better mindfulness and we're more caring to our loved ones.

A study at British Columbia University reported that people said they experienced greater happiness if they used the sum of $40 to save time, by paying for others to complete their chores, than they did if they used it to buy a physical item. So if people who spend money to buy themselves more free time are happier and have higher life satisfaction, it's a good idea to try to bring this into your life. The benefits can be compounded with other sources of happiness, such as giving yourself a sense of community by stimulating your local economy. For instance, hiring in a cleaner not only frees up hours of your time, but you are also supporting the livelihood of someone in your area.

If budget is an issue, you can always try a skill swap. Your friend might be super quick at doing a job which you're very slow at, and vice versa, so perhaps you could do their ironing while they do a repair job for you – and you'll both save time.

Make a list of areas of your life where you could benefit from having outside help.

Think about where in your life you're stuck, or not qualified to solve a problem or deliver a service. For instance, if you feel time-poor, having someone in to clean your house will really give you back some hours, your home will be sparkling and you'll enjoy it more.

If you're feeling financially foggy, perhaps you could hire an independent financial advisor, a business coach or a new accountant who communicates well. If you aren't sticking to your health goals, you could call on a personal trainer, a nutritionist or perhaps a wellness coach. If you're feeling clueless about some of your relationships or struggling with some tougher stuff, it could be time to bring in some good ol' therapy.

Have a think about your skills, and ways you could swap these with your friends and family.

It's taken me a long time to get used to asking for help, I'm definitely someone that loves to do it myself if I can. The success of my business and all the international travel it involved forced me to get creative and outsource certain tasks for the company and at home, and I'm pleased to say I've never looked back.

I love finding services that help me have more time, and ways that give me a shortcut to the results I want. On my list for this month is hiring in a social media assistant because creating posts takes me ages, and testing out a healthy meal delivery service to give us a break from cooking.

TAKE ACTION

Choose one thing from your list and implement it into your life this month.

It's up to you which of these time-saving moves you'd like to make. If this step is scary, just start with the easiest one. If you're feeling particularly run off your feet, go with the option that would save you the most time.

Also, remember that hiring in help isn't a life sentence – you can always cancel your cleaner, stop a subscription, break up with your life coach. You've got nothing to lose, other than maybe a bit of money.

This action doesn't have to be anything costly – perhaps you could start by asking a friend who is knowledgeable about the subject, or lean on family or housemates by asking them to pitch in more with household tasks. Reaching out will not only help you, but it'll also be another opportunity for connection.

I'm going to add a job listing to our website for a social media assistant and share it with our fans, because it would be a shortcut if they already understood our brand. I'm going to research some food delivery options and just give one a try. I'm looking forward to having dinner sorted for me – it will feel like I have a personal chef!

68

Oprah for a day

Time flies while we're on autopilot. With a repetitive daily routine, we sometimes find the days blend together and then think where did this week go? Commutes, work, chores and bad habits can really get you stuck in a rut.

This list helps you take yourself out of your rut and routine by taking a day to live your life like someone you admire. When you use your imagination to craft how you pass your time, it can shake off your own limitations on how you can spend your day.

When thinking of your inspirational person, try to go for someone you know takes good care of themselves. You don't want to emulate a wrinkly rock god from yesteryear.

Choose an inspirational person and make a list of all the aspects that you imagine are a part of their day.

You could take inspiration from real people such as celebrities, your boss or a person you know, fictional people from films or books, or people from history.

My example here is Oprah, who has been a inspiration to me since I was a kid. I love how she really connects with people and asks tough questions, and how she has managed to build such a strong brand while still maintaining a position of heartfelt care for others. So when making my list, I ask myself, 'What would Oprah do'? She'd definitely take good care of herself, connect with her loved ones, probably read and probably lead.

She'd eat a good breakfast, have people around her to assist her in achieving her goals and she'd probably wear a really cute outfit. Her time would be spent on the things she cares about, and efficiently, and she'd leave plenty of room on her schedule to recharge and reflect.

TAKE ACTION

Schedule in one day this month to live like Oprah! Or whoever you chose for your inspiring person.

You could use this day to treat yourself or to adopt a more professional mindset. You could emulate an attitude of success in everything you do. Your clothing choices and how you present yourself on this day can be infused with the spirit of this person.

To live my day like Oprah, I'd start by wearing my cutest outfit and eating a lovely breakfast with lots of fresh fruit. I'd manage my time efficiently and leave space for breaks and big-picture thinking. I'd feel a responsibility to help others and lead by example with my kindness and ability to put others at ease. I'd feel fantastic, and under this reframe a few of my bad behaviours would never be able to creep in. I wouldn't waste my time scrolling through social media, my attitude would stay positive and open, imposter syndrome wouldn't dare cross my mind.

We all have the same 24 hours in a day (well, 16 if you've slept sufficiently), so let's make sure we're spending it in a way we believe is admirable.

69

Explore the world from home

Whether you're a seasoned traveller or a homebody, you have the ability to explore the world right at your fingertips. We are so lucky to have so many sources of information available to us, mostly for free, and we have no excuse not to explore the world from home.

Indulge your wanderlust by listening to music, reading books, watching movies, admiring art, enjoying music and cooking food from all around the world. Experience more beauty, widen your tastes and learn about cultures outside your own.

When we step out of our sameness and enhance our view of all the different styles, flourishes, atmospheres and creativity outside our own culture, we get a sense of global community, and feel more connected to fellow humans as a whole. There is less 'us and them'.

List ten ways you'd like to explore the world through art, music, literature, film and food.

Perhaps there's a specific area of the world you'd like to know more about, or a culture that you'd like to explore. You can choose a faraway place, or a city in your own country that you've always wanted to visit or learn more about.

You can access countless art galleries and museums online, and stream music from a certain place or country. If you have no idea where to start, just do a search like 'most famous artists from Ghana' for instance. There are millions of recipes available to you for free, books that have been translated into your language and millions of videos of traditional dances.

A few years ago I spent a lot of time watching all the Bollywood films I could find on my streaming platforms, and would play them while I attempted to cook classic Indian recipes. It was so much fun. I also love listening to Italian opera while sipping a glass of barolo and making a new pasta recipe.

You can even use a pretend time machine to drill down the experience and choose a specific era or time period in that country or culture. London in the swinging 60s, anyone?

Yeah, baby!

TAKE ACTION

Choose one entry on your list and plan a day to explore it in the next month.

Get a playlist ready to listen to while you're on a walk. Save movies to your favourites, so the next time you log into Netflix you're reminded to expand your horizons instead of re-binging *The Office*. Search for recipes that look delicious and are way different to your usual culinary forays.

You can find free online videos and tours of places, such as a lovely drive through Switzerland, a walk around Positano or a sunset view of Sydney Harbour. You could make a traditional tagine while listening to the latest female pop stars from Morocco, or take a deep dive search on Fabergé eggs while listening to Rachmaninoff and eating borscht.

My husband and I love to do this regularly, and we combine a few mediums at a time to really immerse ourselves. We'll plan a meal from a certain place and play one of the local radio stations while we're chopping and cooking. Sometimes I'll mix a typical cocktail to match, and sometimes we watch a movie from that place or country.

70

Roadblocks

We all get stopped by roadblocks, whether we've set them for ourselves or they were put there by outside forces. A roadblock can prevent us from furthering our career, making new friends or moving forward with a project.

Some roadblocks are easier to overcome than others, such as a lack of information, which can be easily resolved by doing some research or asking some experts. Some roadblocks will never be thwarted and we just have to make a detour.

Defining what stands in the way of success, or simply moving forward, is a really powerful exercise. If you can take the first step of recognizing exactly what is holding you up, you have a pretty good chance of overcoming it and deciding what to do next.

Most of the time, our roadblocks are created by our own selves, which can be good and bad news. If we're holding ourselves back, we have the option to let go, but this can be even harder than overcoming blocks from outside forces. This list is about self-imposed roadblocks, because we have the power to blast them away.

The most obvious roadblock is procrastination, such as never getting out your art supplies and painting. We all get in our own way, so let's identify exactly how.

Make a list the roadblocks in the way of your success in achieving your goals.

You can list mindset- and attitude-related blocks, such as a fear of success or lack of self-confidence. You can also add if you're simply lacking practical information, supplies or equipment.

Perhaps you're too nervous to ask your boss for a raise, or trying to muster the courage to ask out your crush. Maybe you really want to be a science teacher, but don't have the required qualifications. Your dream is to swim with the dolphins, but you can barely doggy paddle.

If you are procrastinating and 'protaskinating', definitely call yourself out and add it to this list. Whatever you are putting off, chances are it's more painful to have this low-level sinking feeling every day you don't take action than actually doing the thing.

I waited a shocking amount of time to get my UK driver's license. I'd already learned to drive in the States and had been driving since I was 16, but it took me about 14 years of living in London before I got around to learning how to drive in the UK. It took a fair amount of courage to brave the left side of the road and all those roundabouts, but I did it!

TAKE ACTION

Focus on removing one of these roadblocks this month.

It's time to throw everything at it! Ask for help from an expert or someone who's done it before. Ask a friend to help you by being an accountability buddy. Create your own accountability by telling everyone you know about what you plan to achieve.

Break it down into small, achievable steps so instead of being a boulder in your way, you can chip off one chunk at a time. If you're trying to gain confidence to ask for a raise or promotion, you could start to work on this by writing down what you'd like to say. This will take it from being a thought and turn it into a plan.

If you can't blast the block in one fell swoop, focus on working towards removing it. If you want to be a stronger swimmer so you can meet some dolphins, sign up for lessons at your local pool.

If you want to superpower your approach, make it uncomfortable to carry on regular life until you clear the roadblock. Put reminders everywhere, have a friend check in on you, don't allow yourself sofa or scroll time until it's done. Be your own taskmaster!

Visualization really helped me take the first step and sign up for driving lessons. I imagined all the fun adventures I could take if I were able to drive in the country I live in. I remembered how fun it was to drive and listen to my favourite music in my youth. Being a city-dweller, I don't use our car often, but having the option gives me such a sense of freedom.

71

Compliment box

We tend to forget all the wonderful comments that we receive from our loved ones, our friends, at work from colleagues and superiors, and even the ones from strangers.

This list will help you get in the habit of remembering and recording the glowing comments you've received, so you can access them when you need a boost.

Make a list of ten compliments you've received and from whom.

You can include any lovely things people have said about your work, your appearance, your personality, or how you handled a situation.

Perhaps you had some great feedback from a colleague or client about a job well done, or a stranger mentioned they liked your T-shirt or jazzy socks. Maybe a family member told you they were impressed with how well you found a solution to a problem. Also, if someone simply said 'You're the best', you can add that too!

Recently my friend told me she loved some advice I gave her, to look after herself first in order to look after others. I was so proud to be able to help her during a trying time in her life, and to receive acknowledgement for that filled my heart. Another compliment I received was from my husband, who said he liked how my hair curls when it dries naturally. I didn't even have to try hard for that one!

TAKE ACTION

Find ways to savour and remind yourself of these compliments on a daily basis.

This is the fun part where you get to bask in all the wonderful things people have said about you. You could add the personal compliment of 'You're so inspiring' to your journal so you see it everyday. You could have a screen saver on your computer displaying a professional compliment you received from your boss or colleague.

Feel free to also add the name to the complimenter next to the compliment, so it reads like a theatre review. For example, 'You look zesty!' – Ffion.

If you find you're not receiving many compliments, start giving them and you'll feel great. They'll roll in before you know it.

Be sure to keep track of any new compliments you get during the next month in a notebook or notes app on a regular basis so you can apply the action step for those as well.

72

Visual influences

Many studies have shown that when we see things, we are more likely to engage with them. The visual environment can play a big role in whether we succeed at reaching our goals or improving our behaviours. Luckily, what's on view at home and at work is something we can control and improve.

This list will help you curate what's in your immediate eye line, and will give you a better chance of engaging with thoughts, behaviours and activities that lead to happiness. Whether it be what's on the counter, where we set down our phones, or the location of your gym trainers, you can adjust what you see to match your goals.

Make a list of everything you see (or don't see) in your home or workspace that doesn't align with your goals.

For instance, if you'd like to be calmer and less anxious, you might jot down the cluttered corner in your bedroom that stresses you out. If you are trying to avoid sugar but have jelly beans on your desk at work, this is likely to be affecting your success.

Perhaps you'd like to add healthy behaviours to your lifestyle, such as yoga or drinking more water, but there's nary a yoga mat or a glass of water to be seen. Add these missing things to your list.

If you're always running late, perhaps you can create a spot by the door for your keys, cards and sunglasses so you have an easy time getting out the house.

I got into the bad habit of missing fitness classes because I was always late. I struggled to find all the stuff I needed to pack into my backpack before a class, and I would leave it until the last minute and be so late that I wouldn't get there on time even if I had a helicopter. I annoyed myself so much that I posted a gym packing list on the door of my wardrobe reminding me to pack the night before. I also moved all my fitness gear, which was previously in the bottom drawer, up to the top drawer so it was really easy to grab. It worked – I'm rarely late these days!

 **T A K E   A C T I O N**

Choose three items from your list to add or take away from your line of vision this month.

Give yourself success by your own design! Carefully curate your home and workspace to fit with your ideal life.

Remove clutter and add easy access to things that will help your success. Feel free to make it beautiful, such as placing a rolled-up yoga mat just so next to a lovely plant. Buy a glass water pitcher for your desk and keep fresh lemons and limes on hand so you can hydrate in style. If you'd like to be more creative, place your art supplies or tools in a place you'll see them often.

On my list, I noted that I would love to play my guitar, but I never get to it because it's usually packed away. So I will place it on a guitar stand in a corner of my bedroom to make it more easily accessible.

73

The dream team

Our lives, on a basic level, are made up of the people and relationships that surround us. As humans, we have a primal need to be accepted and loved within our groups. Instead of focusing on what you can get from the people in your life, this list will help you think about how to cherish your dream team.

Make a list of all the important people in your life – include family, friends and co-workers.

Feel free to separate them into these sections if it makes the exercise easier. Most of us have never made a list of all of these people, even though they are the fabric of what makes our lives meaningful. Interesting, right?

Some of these people might belong to multiple categories, such as a co-worker who has become a close friend, or perhaps you consider a friend to be part of your 'chosen family'.

As an expat, I live thousands of miles away from my family, so I always put lots of time and effort into my relationships with them to make sure we stay close. I am so thankful for my friends, who are scattered across the world, and I express my love for them freely and often. The dreamiest part of my dream team are my husband and my dog here in London – we are inseparable.

Each of these special people deserve my thoughtfulness, care and attention, and it's up to me to show them how important they are to me.

TAKE ACTION

Make a plan this month to spend more time, to help or to chat more often with the members of your dream team.

Reflect on what you can do to strengthen your relationships with each of these people, and reach out to tell them why you're grateful to have them in your life.

Everybody likes to be celebrated in different ways. For instance, I personally would rather have quality time with my friends than a gift sent to my house. I much prefer actions rather than stuff. I always tell my husband that the smoothies he makes me in the morning save my life, otherwise I'd skip breakfast completely. Those smoothies are way more meaningful to me than any gift, and I feel so loved when he makes them.

Gary Chapman's '5 Love Languages' describe how certain people respond more to one or two of the following: Words of Affirmation, Acts of Service, Receiving Gifts, Quality Time and Physical Touch. Prescribe your actions to each loved one accordingly!

Organize activities with your family, friends and co-workers to learn more about each other in different situations and share experiences. How can you make each others' lives even better? For instance, there's always room to be more thoughtful around birthdays, so you could schedule tasks in your calendar to sort out their presents a month in advance.

74

Face your fears

It's a common misconception that courageous people experience less fear than the rest of us. It's actually the other way around, as you become more brave when you regularly face your fears and overcome them. Getting into the practice of overcoming your fears is like a muscle – the more you use it, the stronger you get.

Giving into your fears becomes a problem when you're shielding yourself from potential life enjoyment. Yes, it makes you feel safer in the short term to avoid certain situations, but fear has a sneaky way of showing up at inconvenient times, or gives you a constant low level of anxiety that makes you feel downright yucky. In some cases, it holds you back from reaching your goals and achieving your dreams. Let's declutter this.

Make a list of your biggest fears.

Get them down on paper. You can throw it away or burn it afterwards, but definitely write them down.

The fears we're addressing here can either be smaller ones that cause you annoyance or cramp your style, or larger ones that are deferring your enjoyment of life and success. They're roadblocks that stop us from developing deeper relationships, reaching goals or even worse, from having fun. We've all got 'em, so let's spend some time this month on vanquishing one of them.

Your fears could be around asking your boss for a salary increase, or having the confidence to go to a party where you only know a couple of people, or an overdue trip to the dentist.

Seeing your fears written down will not only make them a bit less scary, but it will help you decipher which of these fears are something you can face, are unfounded or beyond your control.

TAKE ACTION

Face one of these fears in the next month, and map out what it would take to help you overcome it.

If you're afraid of asking your boss for a raise, take a practical approach. Research what the average salary is for your role and buff up your CV by adding your current job and description to it. You'll marvel at how much you've achieved, and this act alone might give you the boost you needed to ask for a meeting.

If you're sheepish about meeting new people, set yourself the intention that one can never have too many friends, put your shoulders back, smile and introduce yourself. If you feel awkward, pay someone a compliment. You'll be having the best time before you know it!

It's so easy to put off a dentist visit, but you could just make the appointment and floss every day until then, or go see the hygienist first to build your confidence. They're professionals and will take good care of your pearly whites.

75

What are you like?

Take a moment to consider how your behaviour may have affected other people today. Having awareness of how the way we act impacts others is important to our understanding of one another and helps us keep an eye on our kindness.

It's easy to become self-focused when we're busy and there are so many distractions around. We're constantly looking at our phones, which sends the signal of 'don't bother me' whether we feel that way or not. We rush around to get from one place or task to another, bumping into each other or walking around with resting bitch face because we're thinking about the next thing.

This list will help you, and people you encounter, to have a more pleasant life experience and allow for the possibility of interpersonal connection.

Make a list of interactions today and how you behaved, such as the energy you emitted and your attitude and demeanour.

Your interactions can include the ones with those on your morning commute, or how you greeted your partner or housemate, had a meeting, bought coffee or took a phone call.

Assess your behaviour, and first look at the facts rather than the feelings, such as if you said thank you, did you smile, were you kind, did you have good manners? Consider your body language, for instance whether you stared at the ground as you walked or took a confident stride with your shoulders back.

Think about your conversations. For instance, if you were helpful to someone, or if you complained a lot, or if you were in a rush and brought stressful vibes into the workplace. When engaging with others, think back to whether you asked how they were, or if you only talked about yourself.

You might face some harsh truths here if you've been on autopilot. This exercise in mindfulness starts with you considering how you approach your actions with others, but equally will involve how you react to others who are not being mindful of their behaviour or lacking kindness.

 **T A K E   A C T I O N**

Take a day this week to be mindful of your behaviour with other people.

If you're aware of the way you present yourself, you'll take a bit more care when interacting with others. This awareness will help you hone your behaviour so that you are not a source of negativity for those you interact with.

Consider how you can inject more thoughtfulness, gentleness, humour and care into the way you interact with people. Once you've paid attention to the behaviour you're putting out into the world, it will get easier and easier to be polite and positive, and this attitude will inspire others to do the same.

Kindness is contagious and it starts with you!

76

A walk in the park

Research has shown that we feel more at ease when we are surrounded by nature instead of a city setting. Noisy streets cause heightened stress levels, whereas our brain waves relax when we're in a quieter park setting. There have been plenty of studies to prove that the more time you spend in green space, the happier you feel.

Walking amongst green grass, plants and trees improves your mood and self-esteem, even from exposure for shorter periods of time. So try to fit in a short walk regularly, and have nearby routes ready to be explored. With this list, you'll identify your go-to ways to get a chlorophyll fix in your local area.

Make a list of peaceful, green, quieter places to walk regularly, when you need reflection or just a breath of fresh air.

You can simply make a list of your local parks in order of geographic closeness, or choose places you love. If you've not visited any local parks, you can look online, and maybe even see ratings from people in your community.

If you're fortunate enough to have a backyard or garden, you can take regular walks around it to survey your plants and trees, and maybe even say hello to them! There are plant-identifying apps you can use if you'd like to learn their names.

Having this list compiled and ready to go will make it easier for you to bring in the habit of spending time amongst nature.

TAKE ACTION

Schedule in time to take weekly walks at one of the locations mentioned for the next month.

Going for walks in nature every week will lift your mood, and the exercise will release happiness chemicals in your brain, such as dopamine, and some energizing, depression-fighting endorphins.

It's a good idea to mix up your routes so you don't get bored and lose motivation to get yourself some green. Feel free to invite friends for these floral or forest forays!

One of the best things about living in London are all the beautiful parks right in the middle of the city. Having a dog means we spend a lot of time in parks throwing a tennis ball. We also love to climb the hills of Hampstead Heath or stroll through the beautifully planted flower gardens of Regent's Park.

Growing up I was lucky to live near a mountain called Sleeping Giant State Park and we'd always hike there as a family. I have so many fond memories of spending time there, I can smell the trees in my mind. Whenever I visit home, I try to go there and recharge myself after a long transatlantic journey.

77

The happy zone

This is a two-part list where you'll define both your strengths and passions, and combine the two to find your 'happy zone', i.e. how you can share your unique gifts with the world and have a great time in the process.

This exercise can be used to find a new career or moonlighting gig, or help you better utilize your strengths, talents and passions in your current role.

Please also use this list for finding activities, hobbies and volunteer roles, because following your passions and pairing them with your skills is a very uplifting experience. You will feel a true sense of purpose, and it's proven that when we use our strengths we are inherently happier. The world will benefit from you finding your 'happy zone'.

Discover your 'happy zone' by making a list of all the things you're good at, and a second list of things you enjoy doing.

List 1: My strengths and talents

My examples:
Getting organized
Making people feel welcome
Helping others
Lightening the mood
Communication
Perseverance
Creativity

List 2: Things I most enjoy doing

My examples:
Throwing parties
Listening to music, singing
Playing games
Making and creating
Connecting with people
Performing, entertaining

TAKE ACTION

Write down ways you can connect these two lists to give your gifts to the world, and have a great time doing it.

When you look at the two lists, your mind will creatively come up with ways to combine the different aspects. The more you connect the two, the better!

Let's say for instance, you added the strength 'working with children' and the passion of 'playing sports'. By combining the two, you may have the idea to coach a kids' soccer team in your spare time, or look into training to become a sports teacher.

As you can see from my entries, I've truly found my happy zone in event design and hosting my *Indeedy Bingo* parties. I still find it fun and delightfully challenging after all these years, and I get lost in creating ways to make the experience more fun for our fans and clients. While my creativity and organization play a big role in my business, my keystone strength for its success is definitely 'perseverance'.

If you're looking to pursue a new career or start your own business, this list can be invaluable. I don't agree with the sentiment of 'do what you love and it'll never feel like work', because I think having the differentiation between work and play is good for you. But I can definitely tell you that doing something you love for work sure makes your work day easier!

78

Move your body

Sometimes our happiness needs a shake-up, like a salad dressing that's been sitting in the fridge for a while. This is completely normal, and as I've mentioned in other lists, happiness is a practice. You likely give your salad dressing a big shake every time you use it!

The quickest way to reinvigorate our happiness is by using our physical bodies to help out our overworking brains by doing what they do best – moving.

This list will help you have some wiggly options on tap to get your blood flowing, raise your serotonin levels, engage your cardiovascular system and put a big smile on your face.

Make a list of five ways you can bring movement into your day.

You can add entries of all kinds to this list, and I recommend you start with your favourites. Perhaps you're partial to jumping jacks or prefer some gentle stretching. You could set yourself free with contemporary dance or prowl around your house like your favourite animal.

Even taking a few minutes every hour to walk around your home or office will bring you benefits, but I'd encourage you to make it more fun than that! I love having a dance break in the mid-afternoon, treating myself to a ten-minute hamstring stretch session after work and taking a brisk walk with the dog at lunchtime.

TAKE ACTION

This month, anytime you feel in a low mood or a bit 'blah', move in one or two of the ways you've described in your list.

You should of course still stick to your regular exercise regime while bringing these activity boosts into your days. This is all about using your body to shift your mind, pull yourself out of stagnancy, and shaking up that happiness salad dressing!

My sister Karen is a yoga instructor and personal trainer, and definitely the most active person I know. She's also one of the happiest people I know – it's almost like she moves around so much that the bad vibes can't catch her!

79

Take yourself on a date

It's important to be able to prove to ourselves that we are in control of our own happiness, it gives us confidence that we can improve our lives. Taking yourself on dates is a great way to enjoy and explore what makes us really happy.

This list helps you celebrate yourself, enjoy your life and have some fun. It will increase your self-worth and make you feel a sense of independence. You deserve to give yourself a day/night to remember!

Make a list of nice things you could do for yourself, as if you were taking yourself on a date.

You could list a date to a lovely lunch at a restaurant you've always wanted to try, or to visit a museum, explore at your own pace and buy yourself something from the gift shop. You could add simpler entries such as walking to a beauty spot in your town to admire the views.

On my list is visiting an art museum and having lunch at the museum café, because for some reason the food at those places is usually delicious. I've also added an entry to go on a picnic with myself; I'd bring a lovely blanket, some delicious picnic snacks and drinks, and a good book to read in the sunlight.

My favourite self-date involves me dressing up, taking myself to a delicious dinner, followed by some musical theatre, and then maybe one last cocktail in a gorgeous luxury hotel bar before getting a taxi home.

TAKE ACTION

Choose one item from your list of date ideas and make it happen in the next month.

You can pick one entry that looks the most fun to you, or one that's easiest to pull off. For instance, my picnic idea is for a sunny day, so I'll hit the museum if it's rainy.

The point here is to start somewhere by going on one date with yourself this month, and build towards taking yourself on regular dates for ongoing self-love.

I regularly take myself on cinema dates, often during the daytime because it feels so naughty to shut the laptop and head out to see a movie. I book one of the VIP seats and get a big box of popcorn. I call it 'Big Boss Film Club'. I like doing this because it doesn't take a lot of planning and I can decide on the day or within the hour if I want to indulge.

I think this is a wonderful method of self-care, and it makes me feel really looked after. In fact, it makes me feel pretty smug for a few days because I'm the perfect date!

80

My favourite treats

Having a handy list of ways to treat yourself will help you remember to give yourself rewards. You can use treats as motivation to reach your goals, and to celebrate all that you've achieved. Giving yourself random treats also boosts life enjoyment and happiness, because it makes us believe there's always something good around the corner.

Our brain loves rewards, and studies prove that the brain's pleasure circuit (called the nucleus accumbens) activates even when we anticipate a reward. You can combine this magic of anticipation with your goals, and use treats to reinforce good habits and behaviours that lead to your success.

Make a list of your favourite treats.

Mix up your list with varied types of treats, such as self-care, material items, experiences, activities, food and drink, and relaxation. These can be delicious things like your favourite kind of chocolate, physical things like a new pair of shoes, relaxation-based treats like a long bubble bath, or experiences such as a spa visit. You can include low-cost or free options such as streaming your favourite film, cooking some comfort food and giving yourself a manicure. Having a bunch of healthy treats on this list is a good idea, but only if they really do feel like rewards.

Remember that just the planning and anticipation of these treats will invoke the pleasure principle, and you'll feel great even before you experience the thing.

On my list is an aromatherapy massage, an afternoon to start a new video game and a beautiful trench coat I've been eyeing.

 **TAKE ACTION**

Plan in three treats from your list during the next month.

You can treat yourself for hard work, for reaching a goal or 'just because'. You could run yourself a luxurious bubble bath on a Friday evening to reward yourself for the work week. Buy those lovely new shoes that will elevate all your outfits as a random reward.

It's important here that you take the time to really savour and appreciate the treats, because then you're more likely to build more of them into your life. Say to yourself, 'I am really enjoying this experience'.

From my list, I'm going to buy that trench coat as a reward for finishing a big project. The afternoon of video gaming will be a random indulgence. The aromatherapy massage will be my self-care treat for this month – this is one of my favourite treats by far and I often use it as motivation to hit a goal.

It's true that there's always something good around the corner, especially when you're the one planning it!

81

Sing it loud

Singing is proven to release endorphins, boost our happiness and reduce stress. The breathing involved with singing increases circulation and cognitive performance, and it can be considered aerobic exercise. Whether you can't carry a tune in a bucket or if you are a virtuosic soprano, singing should be brought into your regular happiness practice.

There's further physical and neurological proof to back this up – the sacculus (a tiny organ in the inner ear connected to pleasure circuits in the brain) responds to the frequencies we emit when we sing.

This list will help remind you to use your voice and lift your spirits.

Make a list of songs you love to sing, or songs you'd like to learn to sing.

These can include your favourite pop songs that you already know by heart, or songs you'd love to be able to belt out in the shower or at karaoke. They can be sad songs, romantic love songs or the joyous anthems of your youth. It's good to add an array of moods and genres to this list so that it matches how you're feeling on any given day. You can list seasonal songs like Christmas carols, My Funny Valentine or Auld Lang Syne, so you know them inside and out when the opportunity strikes.

TAKE ACTION

Commit to singing songs from your list on a weekly basis this month.

Feel free to add your list songs into a playlist that you can listen to whenever you need a mood boost, or to better learn the words for unbridled belting.

The voice is the easiest musical instrument to carry around. You can sing anywhere and everywhere, whether it be at the top of your lungs in the shower, as you do the dishes or into your hairbrush in front of the mirror. You could sing with others and add in some social connection by joining a choir, starting a vocal harmony group, or simply just get yourself to a karaoke night. If you're feeling shy, schedule in some time when you'll be alone and undisturbed so you can warble freely.

You might even find yourself making up your own songs, or coming up with your own tune as you sing against the backdrop of an instrumental. I studied music in university with a focus on jazz, so I'm always improvising and messing with melodies as if I was an instrument playing a solo.

My favourite night out with friends is going to karaoke – I lose myself in the singing, but also I get a strong feeling of joy when hearing others attempt songs. I also have a lot of fun attempting to sing operatic arias in the shower, but it does take practice, often in a different language, so it's not for the faint-hearted!

82

Rituals

Having healthy daily rituals in place will help you create good habits for your wellness and life enjoyment. You already have rituals in practice, such as brushing your teeth before bed or your morning meditation.

Bringing some thoughtfulness and creativity to your life on a daily basis will help you frame your mood for the day and engage in some self-care. It can be a safe moment of solace to reset, or to mark the end of a part of your day as you move into the next.

This list will help you come up with ways to bring more self-care and mindfulness into your everyday, and fold them into your regular happiness practice.

Make a list of some new daily rituals that would make you feel fantastic.

Add entries for quiet moments of reflection, daily self-care habits or regular activities that are fun and inject joy into your day.

Express your own personal style into your entries, because these rituals are purely for your happiness. Rather than adding something to this list you think you 'should' do, approach it with things you want to do. If you'd like to be calmer and more relaxed when you get home from work, you could listen to an uplifting podcast everyday on your way home, or as soon as you get in, drink a big glass of water, put on comfy clothes and reset.

I love journalling while I'm drinking coffee every morning. I just flow with my thoughts and feelings, and it's such an excellent primer for my day ahead. It makes me feel present and like I'm on top of everything.

 **T A K E   A C T I O N**

Choose one of these rituals and add them in once a week for the next month.

If you feel like your chosen ritual is helping you get more enjoyment out of your day, then do it daily. I'm only asking you to try it once a week to start gently, but you might find it's so wonderful and effective that it just has to become your new normal.

If you tried one ritual from your list one week and you weren't so sure about it, try a different one the next week.

Make it easy for your rituals to happen - to help you reset at the end of the day, you can lay out your loungewear in the morning so it's ready for you when you get home.

For my morning journalling ritual, I grab my tablet off its charger while I'm making coffee. I put on some calm music in the background, and put on subtle lighting in my room. I sit cross-legged in bed, take a deep breath and write.

83

Read a book

Yes, I know you're reading a book right now, so the fact that I'm telling you to read a book is very meta. But studies show that when we read books, our stress levels are lowered and we are more relaxed than when listening to music, playing video games or drinking a cup of tea! So right now, you're feeling more relaxed by reading this than if you were listening to Enya. How cool is that?

Reading can bring you a new perspective on life, provide endless inspiration and expand your knowledge on countless subjects. Furthermore, research has shown that reading novels helps us better understand other people, which increases our sense of connection and belonging in the world.

Whether you're reading autobiographies from leaders, practical guides about gardening, literary classics or suspenseful novels, adding reading to your happiness practice will definitely yield great results. This list will help you create your own regular opportunities to devour a book, increase your life enjoyment and learn something new.

Make a list of books you'd like to read.

Ask friends for recommendations, or to borrow their favourite book. Visit your local library and ask the librarian to supply some greatest hits. Look at bestseller lists and choose a few in the genres that interest you.

My reading habits tend to lean more towards non-fiction, I love reading inspirational autobiographies, about philosophy, and self-development books. When I do err from non-fiction, I'll usually go for a classic novel that I haven't read yet, because I'm trying to read them all. This is classic overachiever Virgo behaviour, and I really should explore modern fiction a bit more.

 **TAKE ACTION**

Choose one book off your list and schedule in an hour every week this month for cosy book time.

You deserve this level of relaxation, and this reading ritual can become a very important aspect of your self-care. First, choose your book and get your hands on it. Then, set your weekly hours for reading and commit to them. Be sure to close the door to the room, or tell your household you're taking an hour to read and not to disturb you. Make yourself a cup of tea or your favourite drink, get comfortable and lose yourself in the book.

One way to supercharge the health benefits from reading is to join a book club. Sharing your thoughts as a collective enables social connection, and the accountability factor will certainly get you in the practice of reading!

I'm right there with you. I will commit to reading a new fiction book this month, and I'll set myself up a relaxing book nook with a scented candle and a soft blanket.

84

Talk to strangers

We're conditioned to keep to ourselves in public, especially where I live here in London where people can be quite reserved and some don't even talk to their neighbours. Studies show that people are lonelier than ever before and, not so mysteriously, our loneliness factor has increased with each innovation of our phones.

We often think strangers don't want to hear from us, but studies have proven that both parties are filled with a sense of happiness throughout the experience, and this feeling can last for days afterwards. It's the ultimate mood boost, if a little scary at first, but the payoff far outweighs the fear.

This list will help you gather the confidence to reach out to your fellow humans and make a connection.

Make a list of five ways you'd be comfortable talking to strangers this month.

This might take a bit of courage if you're an introvert, so this is why I'm asking you to make a list of the ways that are easiest to you. It gives you a chance to mentally prepare for the interaction, making you far more likely to carry it out. Start thinking of ice-breakers and questions you can ask to make sure you interact. And when you get the jitters don't forget: the other person definitely wants to connect with you, even if they don't know it yet.

Public transport is a great opportunity for this, if you use it. Also, one of the easiest ways to talk to people is if one of you is walking a dog, it's an instant waggy conversation starter.

If talking to strangers feels unsafe, talk to whoever you'd feel comfortable talking to – you can't go wrong with grandmas!

 **T A K E   A C T I O N**

Challenge yourself once a week this month to strike up a conversation with someone you don't know.

Now that you've got a list of possible interactions, make them happen. You could choose a day of the week, and probably the best day to start is Friday, when mostly everyone is in a good mood! However to start? Simply say hello!

Once you get in the habit of talking to strangers, your confidence will grow, as will your joy. It will become easier to connect, and this connection will positively influence all areas of your life.

I said hello to an elderly man in the street the other day and he stopped and asked me how I was. We went on to have a short conversation about the state of the world, the weather, hope for sun, and then went each on our own way. I had a big smile on my face for ages afterwards.

85

Memory lane

Nostalgia is the ultimate comfort. Our minds love to wander to the past, and in this book I'm repeatedly telling you to stay in the present. However, here's your chance to cuddle up to all of those warm memories from the past and explore them.

There's good reason for this – studies have shown that by simply thinking of good memories from the past, you can increase your happiness levels and be more positive about the future. It's been proven that a bit of nostalgia can bring you joy by making you feel comfort.

Make a list of your top ten favourite nostalgic memories, from your earliest years through to recent years.

I've made the parameters pretty wide here, since recent memories and experiences can feel just as special as those of our youth.

Be sure to include the warmest of memories, from childhood birthday parties to wonderful holidays to memorable meals and good friends.

You might find yourself best remembering the moments that were also captured by photos, which argues the case for being in the habit of taking regular photographs to commemorate your life. You can even include feelings, moods, themes or scenes.

For instance, I often find myself reminiscing about the excited feeling I always had in autumn when walking to the bus stop for primary school, the air was crisp and I loved the smell of the changing leaves in the early morning fog. I looked forward to going to school and seeing my friends, so that anticipation was paired with all these other aspects and is probably why this memory is drilled into my mind. It results in a multi-sensory tableau that I've tried to reenact many times but just can't get there. I'm so grateful I can access it within.

 **TAKE ACTION**

This month, take some time to reminisce on your own, or share these memories with your friends and family, and hear their version of memories from that time.

Bask in that comfy hug of nostalgia by walking down memory lane. Feel every aspect as you remember, and let the emotions flow. You might need some tissues for this process.

If I'm being nostalgic on my own, I love using music to help the memories flood back and I write them down as they come to mind in my journal. Sometimes I find myself really inspired from this, and I end up writing lyrics or poetry to better describe the feelings I get from the memory.

After this practice, I usually end up cooking delicious recipes passed down from my mother and grandmother, because nostalgia from food is one of my favourite ways to honour and remember the people I've lost.

Sharing memories with others and learning different perspectives about stories from our past can be so illuminating, it really helps to have other people fill in the blanks you didn't know were there. You can even record the conversations and anecdotes from the ones you love to make sure you never forget the details, and there's nothing like hearing a story from a loved one in their own voice!

One of my favourite times to reminisce with other people is on their birthdays. We're already celebrating them by marking the occasion with a party, some cake or a video chat, but I also love to talk about my favourite memories from our past together. There's always a funny anecdote that I wasn't privy to, or I learn that the way I reacted to a situation wasn't how I remembered it!

86

Swaps

There may be some negative influences in your life that are affecting you more than you know. It helps to take stock of these and do a gut check on what's possibly bringing you down on a regular basis, so that they can be kept in check or eradicated.

It could be someone in your life that makes you feel bad about yourself, or a habit you'd like to shed, or daily activities you'd rather not engage in.

In the vampire comedy show *What We Do In The Shadows*, the sort of negativity we take on from others is exemplified through the character Colin Robinson, an 'energy vampire'. As the show explains, energy vampires drain their victims by making them feel annoyed, bored or awkward, and they tend to frequent offices, council meetings and open-mic nights. The concept of the 'energy vampire' is hilarious to me, and we can all find real-life examples of this sort of person if we examine our surroundings more closely.

This list will help you clearly identify people, things, behaviours or habits that are negatively affecting you, and help you engage healthier, happier swaps when they strike.

Perhaps you have a co-worker who loves to complain, and you absorb his bad attitude. Think about how you can avoid encountering this, or neutralize it when it happens, and write it in as your swap. Maybe you have a family member who always wants to talk about weight loss and you find it triggering.

Or maybe you find yourself mindlessly reaching for cookies or Chianti, and you regret it the next day. You're totally within your right to reach for either of these things if they bring you happiness, but if you're beating yourself up about it the next day, or if you are breaking a self-promise, notice how this turns into a negative. Your swap could be to reach for a piece of fruit instead.

You're writing your own solutions here, which will help you overcome the negative elements, but also will give you self-empowerment and confidence because you will feel in control of what energy you allow in. Don't forget, you're the boss of you!

 **TAKE ACTION**

Now that you've identified your energy vampires, awful activities and hurtful habits, it's time to put your swaps into action.

For your negative ninny co-worker, you could make a plan to stop his complaining in his tracks by either changing the subject or just walking away. I have come across many an office grouch in my old career, and would neutralize them by saying something positive like, 'Yeah but isn't the weather beautiful today?' and give them a wink. This was a gentle way to remind them not to trash my good mood, and it usually worked.

When your family member wants to talk about weight loss or the latest fad diet, you can simply change the subject, or tell them you'd rather talk about something else.

If it's the cookies and Chianti, maybe set yourself up for success by having a healthy treat on hand that you truly find delicious, so you don't get mad at yourself the next day. How about strawberries and sparkling water?

Because you've made a plan, these negative influences no longer have power over you. Your positive swaps will not only make you happier, but you'll be leading by example to others, and proving to yourself that you are indeed the architect of your mood.

87

Happiness, but make it fashion

You might think this list is a bit basic, but I promise you if you embrace it, you will feel as fabulous as you look. Research shows that the way we dress impacts how we feel and is linked to our moods, and that choosing to dress like we would when we're happy can even trick us to feel that way.

A lot of us only dress our best when we're in a good mental state and wanting to have fun, but now it's time to do this the other way around and reverse engineer some joy.

If you think about how you perceive others in public, the people who are wearing dark colours might seem a lot less approachable than someone who is wearing something light, bright and colourful. This list will help you dress to match the mood you'd like to be in, and will engage your creative expression, for compounded happiness.

Make a list of the outfits, articles of clothing and accessories that make you happy when you wear them.

You can choose clothes that have a sentimental value or items that fit perfectly and make you feel great. You can add cheerful colour pops to match or clash the season – whatever boosts your mood and represents positivity to you.

Try to aim for bold patterns and bright colours. Go through your wardrobe and pull out the items that make you feel fabulous and the best version of yourself. Remember to accessorize your outfits, and peruse your jewellery drawer, your colourful scarves, bags, belts, shoes and statement socks.

 **T A K E A C T I O N**

Make a plan to wear these happiness outfits at least three times in the next month.

No matter how you feel on your chosen days, get yourself into these clothes and get ready to feel better. You don't need a special occasion to wear your favourite items, simply being alive is occasion enough! If this exercise made you feel you need more colour in your closet, don't fret. Now you know what to look for when you're shopping, and you likely won't buy another grey hoodie. If budget is an issue, then slowly inject new pieces into your wardrobe when you can.

One of my favourite things to wear is a brightly coloured suit jacket, they make me feel like a confident, creative businesswoman. One of these was passed down to me by my grandmother, an 80s blazer with big shoulder pads in a zingy fuschia pink – a colour my family refers to as 'Grammy Pink'. When I wear it, I feel unstoppable.

Don't forget, the best accessory to any outfit is a beaming smile!

88

Don't be perfect

Trying to be perfect is exhausting, and totally stunts your creativity. Striving for perfection can make you stop you before you start, decrease your productivity and even block personal connections. We bring this pain on ourselves, and continue to do so until we see it for what it is – self-sabotage.

So many of us wait until we feel like it's the perfect timing, or we're the perfect weight, or we're wealthy enough before we allow ourselves to feel true enjoyment. The problem is, this notion of perfection isn't real. We make these unspoken deals with ourselves, and what ends up happening is that we never feel worthy of loving our lives.

Finally, perfection is boring. Showing your vulnerability and imperfections helps you make a heart connection to others, because they see you as a real human being.

This list gives you permission to be happy with your life as it is now, and shed all those parameters bouncing around in your mind. It's time to freely express yourself, follow your dreams and overcome the perfection blocks.

Make list of ways you can embrace the imperfection in your life.

Perhaps you're not the best dancer, or you hide yourself from social media because you're too shy about your appearance.

Maybe you're not a talented artist, but would love to paint or sculpt. Perhaps you'd like to turn your passion for gardening into a business, but you feel you lack expertise.

Just because you're not good or perfect at something doesn't mean you should avoid doing it, exploring it further and enjoying yourself. Everyone has to start somewhere!

 **TAKE ACTION**

Choose three ways from your list and celebrate or engage your imperfect self this month. Do it anyway!

You can dance like no one's watching, post a candid selfie, sculpt anyway. See the beauty in all of these imperfections. I encourage you to start before you feel ready. What's the worst that can happen?

It won't be the end of the world if you feel embarrassed about being less than perfect – you'll get over it. You'll feel so proud of yourself for going for it, far outweighing any regret.

Whenever I feel like I'm not 'ready' to start a creative project, I think of a certain unlikely creative hero. Pigcasso is an artist based in South Africa who creates abstract paintings. Pigcasso is also a pig that paints with her snout! This painterly porcine creates with wild abandon, all while raising large sums for her home, Farm Sanctuary. Let's all be more like Pigcasso!

89

Make the first move

We all have dreams, great hopes, interests we'd love to pursue and life goals we long to achieve. It's too easy to stay safely in your comfort zone and never even take the first step towards these things. Sometimes it's just laziness, or procrastination, or bad self-talk that's getting in your way.

I'll bet in your heart you've already thought of a few dreams or interests you've put on hold for one reason or another, and you probably just need a gentle nudge in the right direction to get you going.

Here is your gentle nudge, my friend. Let's get after those goals.

Make a list of ways you can take the first step of initiative towards your interests, dreams and goals.

If your interest is acting, you can add entries for taking up acting lessons, researching local acting schools and looking for performances happening near you for inspiration.

If you've always wanted to become a vet, your first step could be applying for a veterinary medicine programme, or at least researching the steps to get your veterinary qualification. You could also work part time or volunteer at a veterinarian's practice to 'try on' the career.

Perhaps you want to create some passive income streams, so you can make money in your sleep. This is a wonderful concept to think about but unless you make some moves, it will remain a concept. You could create downloadable content to sell, research investment property, buy some vending machines or rent out your parking space to a commuter.

 **TAKE ACTION**

Choose one item from your list and commit to taking the first step towards it this month.

The best part about this list is that you've already come up with some juicy ways to take action, and now you just have to put one into practice. Stop waiting, now is your time!

Sign up for that acting class, get in touch with your local vet and ask about volunteering, create a downloadable how-to guide for something in your expertise.

If you've been holding yourself back from making a move, perhaps it would help to ask yourself why you're waiting. Maybe you're lacking the confidence, information, time or money to pursue it. Consider what's within your control, and find a way to get started. Once you take the first step, you'll have more momentum as you approach the next steps towards following your dreams.

90

Describe your fantasy dream home

This list is a lovely mix of creative expression and dream exploration. Our desires define who we are, and mentally designing your dream home provides a 'window' to how we truly want to enjoy our lives. Knowing what you want for your dream home helps you know what to aim for, and stretching for big goals will keep you motivated while you reach for all the stepping stones in between.

Using your creativity and imagination to create living spaces makes you feel the effects of the various aspects as you think of them. Imagining your beautiful infinity pool makes you feel peaceful, seeing your walk-in closet full of gorgeous clothes makes you feel luxurious and empowered.

Make a list of all the wonderful aspects of your dream home.

The point here is to dream big and explore your exponential possibilities. Use this list to inspire your wildest imagination of how you'd like your home to be.

Go through each room and list out the details. You can use all your senses as you make this list, such as the feeling of a warm breeze coming from the open French doors that lead out to your veranda. You can feel the soft carpet under your feet as you choose your favourite dress and shoes from your walk-in closet.

On my list, I always include a large entertaining space because I love to throw parties. This likely stems from my matriarchs who made birthdays, holidays and celebrations so memorable. I also always list really specific aspects such as a huge central hallway with a circular table boasting an urn filled with a hundred peonies!

 **TAKE ACTION**

Consider the aspects of your dream home, and decide which of the items you could bring into your life right now.

For instance, if you listed a heated infinity pool because you're yearning for more relaxation, you could visit your local lido or flotation spa and get this experience right now. Or take more lovely bubble baths at home!

Perhaps your wardrobe is overloaded and feels far from luxury. Maybe it's time to declutter some of your clothing that is worn out or doesn't fit perfectly, giving the clothes you keep more space to breathe. Choosing outfits from a jam-packed closet is never easy, so this is a small step towards that luxurious feeling you had in your vision.

Instead of an urn of one hundred peonies, I could buy myself a dozen to lift my surroundings this week. I don't have the entertaining space I dream of right now, but I could have a couple of friends over for dinner and cook them an epic meal and plan some fun entertainment activities the same way I would have if I was in my dream home.

91

Inspire yourself

There are no excuses to be uninspired when we have so many free tools at hand. We use the internet as a reference for all things creative – making art or music or poetry, finding recipes, craft projects, making your own eco-friendly household cleaning products, interior decorating tips, how to start your own company, colour your hair or save a dying houseplant...

Furthermore, most of us have bookshelves full of incredible stories, muses, information, guides and biographies. But sometimes all of this access to knowledge can be overwhelming, so we avoid delving in. This list will help you provide inspiration for yourself, in a constantly renewing and reliable way.

Make a list of how you want to be inspired.

Pay special attention to the areas of your life that you feel need more knowledge, dynamism, colour or energy. Are there aspects of your life that you feel need more growth?

If you're wanting to explore more art, and you happen to see some art you like, you could research the artist and their history, and even perhaps their peers and movement. If you are feeling uninspired about your career, and would like more advancement, then you could re-ignite your interest by looking into the history of the profession, or thinking of all of the people that benefit from it. You could follow leaders in your industry on LinkedIn and let their enthusiasm stoke the fire a bit – you may even start feeling competitive!

One of my favourite ways to find creative inspiration with music is to listen to internet radio or Spotify recommendations. Hearing new stuff and mixing it in with nostalgic favourites definitely spurs me on to write lyrics and melodies. I even love it when their algorithms get me completely wrong as it's always good to try a new listening path.

TAKE ACTION

Choose one item from your list and explore it with a view to seeking some inspiration this month.

Get in the practice of being inspired, and strengthen your ability to find inspiration everywhere. The magic of this list lies in your adventurous discovery, and your self-awareness will be a key factor so you can catch yourself when you get the 'blahs'.

Drilling down the subjects that you crave more inspiration for will help you better seek out a proverbial muse. If you're interested in modern art, you could visit actual museums or their extensive online galleries and libraries of information about various artists. If you're interested in manga, you could visit your local library and borrow books that pique your interest.

Finding inspiration can be really simple if you let it, by using what you've already got. Re-examining your book collection, saved resources on your laptop or revisiting your notes from past courses can all remind you of how far you've come and reinvigorate your inspiration going forward.

92

Back to basics

We are constantly learning about what's new and next, and our society and social media bombard us with the hottest trends in entertainment, fashion and fitness. These crazes come and go so quickly that our heads spin, and we wonder why there are so many butt-lifting leggings in our drawer.

While it's exciting to get involved in all this newness, it can be easy to forget the things we love to do, watch, wear, admire. If you listen to your own tastes and preferences, you can drown out all that noise and go after the activities you really enjoy, and have enjoyed for a while. This list is all about appreciating what you already know and love. The tried and true!

Make a list of five things to do that you truly love.

How do you truly enjoy yourself? It doesn't have to be cool. You could add an entry for simply sitting and listening to your favourite music, or embrace your inner child and do some colouring in. Get nostalgic if you want, and think of how you spent your time when you were a bit younger. Perhaps you played a certain game with friends, or made collages and dream boards with photos cut out from magazines. Perhaps you like to wear your best vintage clothing and spend a night on the town.

For me, a good example of this is list-making, which I've always found joyful since I was a teenager. It's my happy place.

TAKE ACTION

Schedule in a session for one of your entries this month to engage in what you love.

Set aside some time to give your true self the fun and enjoyment you truly deserve. Feel the sense of play, care and joy in catering to your inner self on your own terms.

Make sure you have the needed equipment or supplies if you're doing something more involved than listening to your favourite album from 1998. You could treat yourself to a colouring book and a pack of coloured pencils, get stuck in and let your worries float away. Unearth your chessboard and challenge a friend to a match. Dress up in your best vintage outfit and go out and be seen, you absolute work of art!

When I first had the idea to turn my passion of list-making into a nightlife event, something just felt right. It wasn't the coolest or newest thing out there, but I knew that I loved making lists so much that my enthusiasm would be contagious, and I was right. You never know what great things can come from following what you love!

93

Top five funniest moments of your life

Thinking of the funniest moments of your life is an instant mood-booster, and will bring a big smile to your face. Real-life hilarity is usually way funnier than expertly written comedy and blooper reels, and these experiences can help us form a close bond with the other people involved.

Laughter releases happy chemicals in your brain, relieves stress, boosts the immune system and is used as a treatment for depression. It's a good thing if you can conjure up lots of moments from your past when you laughed harder than you imagined you could. Now's the time you get to relive these and reap the ridiculous benefits.

Make a list of the top five funniest moments of your life.

Your entries can include embarrassing moments, funny people, pet behaviours and slapstick-level whoopsies. There will be hilarious family situations, shockers from school, epic fails and silly misunderstandings.

One of my funniest moments is from when I was six years old. My mom had baked two dozen bread rolls on Christmas Eve and left them to cool on the counter while we went to my grandparents' house for festivities. When we got home, only half of them were left on the counter, and not a crumb in sight. We assumed our dog Curly had eaten them and it was going to be a rough night looking after her. My mom was pretty annoyed.

When it was time to put me to bed, my mom came in and started to remove all my dolls from on top of my pillows and found... twelve bread rolls! My mom looked at me in horror thinking I had stolen all these rolls (I did love them), but shortly afterwards she realized Curly had somehow carried them all upstairs and stashed them in my bed behind my dolls! What a clever and naughty dog. I was framed! Mom called all the family in and we laughed so hard, and we still do about this story.

 **TAKE ACTION**

Take a minute to remember these moments, and have yourself a big chuckle.

Having this list on hand is a great help when you need to lighten your mood. Reminiscing is a healthy habit anyway, as it increases your life enjoyment and makes you feel more secure. Mixing this in with laughter is a very unique cocktail and will have you giggling as hard as you did the first time around.

Feel free to call up a friend and share the story with them, because everyone wants their friend to call them with a funny story.

94

Instant self-care

We don't always have time for long, drawn-out luxurious self-care practices, but that doesn't mean we can't look after ourselves. With only a little bit of planning, or simply reorganizing what's at the ready, we can bring the act of taking good care of ourselves into our daily lives.

Taking good care of yourself will give you more confidence, a higher sense of self-worth and increase your productivity. It's in everyone's best interests for you to look after yourself!

This list will help you set yourself up for regular self-care throughout your day.

Make a list of five ways you can engage in self-care easily and instantly.

You could start by thinking of where you spend your time and how you can make your self-care habits easily accessible. You're more likely to do these things for yourself if they are at your fingertips.

For instance, if you spend a lot of time in an office, you could keep a really lovely hand lotion on your desk, and keep your hands looking and feeling well looked-after. At home, you could keep a relaxing aromatherapy spray on your bedside table to spritz on your pillow before you sleep, to maximize your rest.

The easiest self-care practice you can do is mindful, deep breathing – you can do this anywhere and mostly anytime, and the physical and mental health benefits are many.

 **TAKE ACTION**

Add these self-care moments into your life at least once a week this month.

Usher your favourite hand lotion on your desk at work, and a lovely pillow mist on your bedside table. Put a sticky note on your computer that says, 'Breathe', which will help you feel cool as a cucumber all day.

I have a little 'vitamin bar' at a very easy-to-reach place in my most accessible kitchen cupboard. I buy a mixture of gummy vitamins and supplement sprays to make it super easy for me to take, and their front and centre location reminds me to take them daily.

95

Plan a holiday

Making future plans to relax not only helps reduce stress levels when we get to our destination, but it increases our happiness in the lead-up to the trip. Some research has shown that simply planning a vacation increases our happiness more than the vacation itself, and its positive effects can last up to eight weeks.

It's all about the anticipation of the trip, so that means we should plan regular holidays for ourselves. Booking these trips is money well spent, because we are more likely to excitedly talk to others about our experiences than material purchases.

Make a list of all the places you'd like to visit on holiday this year to completely relax and have fun.

This list will be different from your 'bucket list' destinations, I want you to think of places to go that are within your reach this year. If your budget is tight, this could include city breaks or camping trips. If you've been saving up for a big vacation, you can add farther-flung places that you've always wanted to visit. You could start doing your research on costs now, and budget accordingly.

If you're starting from scratch, you could help trigger some ideas by thinking of what your ideal setting would be, such as long sandy beaches, or majestic mountainscapes, or a theme park with the fastest rollercoasters.

I can definitely say I'm happier when I have trips to look forward to in my calendar. City breaks are probably my favourite, I love to research and visit local restaurants, and I'm like a detective when I'm searching for the best drag shows and karaoke bars. I always take in the contemporary art museums and galleries, and make sure I visit historic parts of the city and admire its architecture.

 **TAKE ACTION**

Choose one place from your list and take steps to either book it, budget for it or plan it with others.

Get ready to feel the buzz of vacation planning! Choose the destination and start looking for places to stay. Consider the area of the place you'd most like to be in, for optimum exploring or a shorter walk to the beach. Research the local food scene and its restaurants and read their menus. You can even start on your packing list, and plan yourself some fierce outfits!

I'm lucky to travel so much with *Indeedy Bingo*, and because my team are also my friends it's like we're constantly going on city breaks. My organization skills definitely come in handy here, and I plan lovely meals and drinks for us at cool places. Sometimes my itineraries are tight, especially on a show day, but I try make sure we get the most out of our trips, with plenty of down time too.

For longer vacations, I'm less detailed and plan loose themes like 'travel day', 'beach day' or 'long hike and picnic'. For these trips, I usually choose a beautiful nature setting and I really unwind.

96

Snap out of it

Sometimes we just don't feel like doing the things we've committed to do, like going to work, attending a social event or going to the grocery store. The thing is, our bad attitudes can talk us out of honouring these commitments, and ultimately block us from reaching our goals.

You need to work to earn money to pay the bills. You want to make more friends and have more fun, so you said you'd be going to that party. You dread going to the grocery store, but you've got to make yourself dinner. I get it, my inner self can be a brat too. But that's when it's time to... snap out of it!

Getting out of your own way and achieving the tasks you've set out for yourself is a vital part to maintaining your happiness and feeling successful. This list will help you avenge your own worst enemy and save your best friend – yourself!

Make a list of five ways you can get yourself to snap out of it when you're in a bad mood or feeling stuck.

Perhaps you could find a way to give yourself perspective, such as considering how grateful you are to have work, and how lucky that you've been invited to a party. You could make a deal with yourself to go out and help someone during the experience, such as helping an elderly person bag up their shopping at checkout.

Some moods will require more heavy lifting than others, so it's good to have a few levels of reboots here. For me, sometimes just drinking a big cold glass of water gets me out of my funk. Other times, I need to bring in the big dogs and blast my Disco Divas playlist to get me out of the house and off to that party. Often times, what I really need is just a quick nap or meditation to brighten my outlook and face the busy grocery store.

TAKE ACTION

This month, change your attitude as needed by engaging in one of the tricks on your list.

Put this list somewhere visible, and perhaps in the room or place where you're most likely to have a feeling of stuckness. I keep lists like these on my bedroom mirror, in my wardrobe or for maximum unavoidability, on my fridge door.

Keeping these resets at hand will help you when the negativity sets in, and give you a quick solution to getting over yourself and sticking to your commitments. As you prove to yourself that you happily do what brings progress to your life, you'll have a better sense of self-efficacy and you'll feel a lot more satisfied with yourself.

97

The magic wand

What would you do if you couldn't fail? Let's pretend I have a magic wand that will grant the achievement of even your most far-reaching goals. Let your imagination flow. This list could have easily been titled 'come up with some big goals', but sometimes a prompt or question that is framed in a different way inspires you come up with more creative answers.

I want to see you reach higher than ever before and out of your comfort zone.

Make a list of all the things you would like to achieve in your life, with the confidence that you will definitely be successful.

For instance, you can include personal goals of running a marathon, or being able to play all the jazz standards from *The Real Book* on piano. You can add professional goals such as becoming CEO of your company or owning a bed and breakfast to this list.

According to a study at Dominican University in California, even the simple act of writing down your crazy goals makes them 42% more achievable. Think big, because we're about to break through some barriers here.

I love making this list because dreaming big and setting goals are some of my favourite things to do. On my list I often include having my own television and radio network that programmes only fun, uplifting shows and practical how-tos. Other entries have included being able to dance like Janet Jackson, owning my own private island in a warm climate and writing a book that helps people find happiness through list-making (not so unachievable after all!).

TAKE ACTION

Make a map of what steps you'd need to take in order to achieve these goals. Do you need any more education, qualifications, knowledge, training, luck?

If it's about knowing the right people or being in an industry, can you take part in networking events or find a way to be a part of that world? For instance, if you want to be able to run a marathon, perhaps you would research training regimes online and schedule them into your calendar. Some of your entries will be easier than others, for instance the path to becoming a brain surgeon would take a lot longer than becoming a wedding planner.

This task gets you to think outside of yourself and your immediate reality. You have nothing to lose when it comes to this list. If you follow the paths on your map you will always gain more knowledge and experience, and you'll learn more about your preferences and hone in on what you really want.

98

Child's play

In our adult lives, we can be far too focused on our careers, money and ambitions, and it's so easy to forget to live in the moment and just have fun. We can learn a lot from children, their bounding energy, their excitement over the little things, their innocence and their wild imaginations. They're not afraid to get messy and they don't try to be perfect.

Take some time to remember the things that brought you joy as a child. Recording them into a list will make you feel warm and nostalgic, and remind you of happy feelings from your youngest years.

This list will help you come up with ideas to give you a break from 'adulting', so you can be present in the now and have some fun!

List ten ways you can engage your inner child.

You can add to your list ideas inspired by your own childhood, as well as including activities you'd wished you got to do when you were a kid.

Your entries don't all have to be active ones, for instance you could list something simple and quiet such as colouring in, or just sitting and spacing out while you watch dust particles in a ray of sunlight. I used to do that a lot!

I remember when I was a kid, my neighbourhood friends and I used to invent new games all the time using a football, or innovate on the rules of tag. We'd build an igloo out of snow in winter and put cans of soda and snacks in it – it felt more like a house if it had food in it! In summer I'd just lay in the grass on the front lawn and try to count the leaves above me.

 **TAKE ACTION**

Choose an item on your list and plan to have some fun this month!

Take some time to feel that special brand of childhood happiness by engaging in one of the activities from your list. If you can't decide which one to go for first, choose the one that gives you the biggest jolt of joy.

You could gather some friends for a game of tag or musical statues in your local park. You could calm your active mind with some finger painting, or buy yourself a fresh pack of brightly coloured clay and lose yourself.

When I was kid, my dad built us a trapeze zip-line contraption in our backyard called a 'space trolley'. We spent hours going back and forth on this thing, and we'd take turns trying to race alongside to outrun it. I remember being so out of breath, but so very happy.

99

Eat the rainbow

We've been told to eat our fruit and veggies from a young age, and of course we know it's good for our nutrition and physical health. People who maintain diets rich with these foods are known to live longer, avoid disease and enjoy a higher quality of life.

Recent studies prove that eating eight portions of fruit and veg a day also benefits our psychological health and wellbeing. Increased happiness is linked with eating your greens, and research has shown that the mood-boosting effects are immediate.

Getting into the habit of incorporating lots of fruit and vegetables into your meals is such a good idea, and it's an inexpensive way to ensure the health of your body and mind. This list will help you eat the rainbow.

Make a list of ten ways you could bring more fruit and vegetables into your diet.

You can add entries to your list for trying new types of fruit and veg that you've never tasted before. You can add some healthy swaps such as having courgetti noodles instead of pasta. You could think of ways to help yourself reach for the healthy stuff, such as keeping a beautiful bowl of oranges on your counter, or chopping up veg for the week to make it easier to throw together salads, soups and easy snacks.

One of my favourite ways to add more good stuff into my diet is by drinking smoothies. We throw bananas, kale, berries, protein powder and flax oil into the blender, and the result is delicious. I'm on my way to eight portion-a-day happiness before 10am.

 **TAKE ACTION**

Choose three fruit and veg ideas from your list and plan them into your meals this month for maximum happiness and life satisfaction.

Now that you've thought of ways to bring all this colour, nutrition and mood-boosting food into your life, it's time to make it happen.

Make a shopping list and pick up all of the items required. Or you could visit a market or veg stand and buy whatever looks interesting and delicious to you. Research some recipes online to help you mix a variation of fruit and vegetables into your meals.

Feel free to try different ways of preparation and cooking because the process will affect the flavours. Brussels sprouts are not nearly as tasty boiled as they are when they are roasted, the latter method turns them into nutty, melt-in-your mouth flavour bombs.

I sneak some extra fruit into my day by mashing a banana with cacao powder, a trick I learned from my sister Kiki. It's a great solution to an evening chocolate craving!

100

Cherish

We often focus too much on the future, striving for the things we want and thinking our lives will be better when we purchase or achieve something. The fact is, these moments and feelings we're chasing are accessible now. Everything around you is a product of your past successes, achievements, hard work, chance meetings, love, care, collecting and legwork.

This list will help you realize how wonderful your life is now, and encourage you to feel complete fulfilment with what you've already achieved.

Make a list of items, people, pets and aspects of your life that you'd love to spend more time cherishing.

You can list the various people in your life that bring you so much love, fun and adventure. Perhaps you're so grateful to live in your city or neighbourhood and you could spend more time appreciating it.

Maybe you bought an objet d'art when travelling and it's living in a box under your bed. Perhaps you have a cute cat but haven't spent much time curled up together lately.

For my list, I added my whole family, my friends, my husband Charles, my dog Marlowe, and specific possessions that have a sentimental importance in my life such as my mother's paintings and my grandmother's blazers.

TAKE ACTION

Take some time to love and cherish these items, people, pets and aspects of your life.

Set aside time over the next month to carry out your appreciation for these wonderful things in your life. You can express the act of cherishing by spending more of your time with the item or person, taking a moment to admire and revel in it, or use it more regularly.

Perhaps you can better display a vase or an artwork that you've collected in a place where you'll see it more often. You could stage a little photo shoot for your cat and capture her beauty. You could write a lovely note to a friend or family member and tell them how much you appreciate them.

I love this exercise, because it makes us so thankful for what we've already got, and reflect on how much we've achieved. Let's enjoy everything we've brought into our lives.

I recently spent an hour cleaning all the jewellery I've collected over the years. This task may seem mundane on the outside, but as I washed and polished each piece, memories flooded back. I thought of where I bought these pieces or if they came to me as gifts from friends and loved ones, and remembered so many fun and special times I had while wearing them. I felt so happy after this introspection, and now all my jewellery is sparkling like new.

Acknowledgements

To Charles, my soulmate, husband, best friend, business partner, and ultimate sounding board. You're the most loving dreamboat, and I'm so lucky to be spending my life with you. You relax and inspire me at the same time. Thank you for keeping me well-fed and watered while I wrote, and enduring my process of reading everything aloud. You're always at the top of my list, I love you.

Deep gratitude to my late matriarchs, my mom Betti and grandmother Bertha, who taught me to put love into everything I do. These women exemplified organized creativity and showed me how lists can be used to run a home, plan epic celebrations, and bring happiness to myself and to others. To my whole family: my dad Chris (my biggest cheerleader), my sister Aimee, my brother Chris II, and a big thanks to my sister Karen (aka Kiki) who was a constant source of love and support as I wrote this book.

To my best mate Jim Donahue, who has been my list-making partner and creative muse since we were teenagers. Your encouragement and friendship mean the world to me.

To my dear *I Love Lists* and *Indeedy Bingo* fans, your support enables me to express myself through events. From the old guard to the newbies, thanks for having fun with me!

To my Indeedy family: Ffion, Jenny, Sarah (DJ Klankbad), Soo Mee, Maz, Dani Deluxe, Dom (DJ Speedy), Sonia, Vicky, Cerys, Angela, Sian and Romayne. You're the wind beneath my bingo wings!

Special thanks to the multi-talented and sunny Ffion who was so helpful during the yearlong making of this book, both professionally and through friendship.

To Susan at MBA, my fellow list enthusiast. Thanks for catalyzing this project and seeing the possibility of turning my passion into a book! To Harriet, Katherine and the team at Quadrille for bringing this book into the world. Working with you has been a delight.

To Amanda and Nick, for their friendship and support; especially Amanda for her guidance and literary votes of confidence.

To Katey, Dom, Isaac, Bextacular, Alex, Joyce and Nicky Fusco, my friends for the long haul.

To my confidantes in Wine Club: Didi, Sorcha, Katy, Kelsey, Maura, and especially Tica who rooted for me at every step.

To Vanessa at Soho House, who saw potential way back in 2009 when I pitched my idea for a little list-making night for the club. May the adventures never end!

To my therapist Nicole, for helping me navigate life with utter enjoyment. And to all the scientists, doctors and researchers who carried out studies on human happiness that informed this book.

And finally, to my fur son Marlowe, who adorably snoozed on my feet throughout the creation of this book and was always ready for cuddle breaks. Thank you for reminding me to be in the moment and for always making me so happy.

PUBLISHING DIRECTOR Sarah Lavelle
JUNIOR COMMISSIONING EDITOR Harriet Webster
SENIOR DESIGNER Katherine Keeble
ILLUSTRATOR Basia Stryjecka
HEAD OF PRODUCTION Stephen Lang
PRODUCTION CONTROLLER Katie Jarvis

Published in 2021 by Quadrille,
an imprint of Hardie Grant Publishing

Quadrille
52–54 Southwark Street
London SE1 1UN
quadrille.com

ISBN 978 1 78713 811 7
Printed in China